Confident Rider Confident Horse

Build YourConfidence and Develop a True Partnership with Your Horse from the Ground to the Saddle

Anne Gage

Revised 2018

Published by Endellion Publishing
Mono, Ontario, Canada

Copyright © Anne Gage 2013

Disclaimer of Liability

The author and publisher shall have neither liability nor responsibility to any person or entity with respect to any loss or damage caused or alleged to be caused directly or indirectly by the information contained in this book. While the book is as accurate as the author can make it, there may be errors, omissions, and inaccuracies.

Photography by: Anne Gage & Deborah Wilson

Diagrams: Anne Gage

ISBN: 978-0-9881359-6-3

DEDICATION

This book is dedicated to my husband, Doug Gage, and to my mother, Joan Lowcock and in loving memory of my father, Kenneth Lowcock.

Thank you for your ongoing support and encouragement.

CONTENTS

Acknowledgements

I am fortunate to be able to make my living doing what I love – working with horses, teaching riders, and providing personal development. The road has not been straight nor has the journey always been easy. I am thankful for the people who have influenced, guided and supported me along the way.

My parents, although somewhat bewildered by my passion for horses, have always been my biggest supporters and unconditionally encourage me to pursue my dreams.

My amazing husband, Doug. He has maintained his sense of humour, lust for life and tolerance for my "hobby" for over 30 years. I honestly could not have done it without him by my side. He has always supported my endeavours and encouraged me to step out of my comfort zone to pursue my dreams.

Chris Irwin, my friend and mentor, has shown me a whole new way to be with horses. The experience has been life changing setting me on a whole, new journey of self discovery. What a ride it has been so far.

Zeke O'Connor, Mike Newell, and Lisa MacFarlane - the people who provided the first opportunities for me to be with and learn about horses, their care and training.

My clients and friends, who support me, challenge me and keep me looking for answers. I am particularly thankful to Marie Balogh and Misha Dubbeld. And the special group who provided feedback and editing suggestions as this book was written – Faye Salsman, Gina Geick, Alison Graham, Kristie Swing, Kelly Jacobsen, and Deborah Wilson (who also provided many of the photographs).

i

Last but certainly never least, I am grateful to all the horses who have been and continue to be my greatest teachers. I did not always get the horse I wanted, but I always got the horse I needed.

None of this would be possible without them.

Introduction

This book is a guide for anyone who is experiencing fear or loss of confidence around horses or in horse related activities. Fear and loss of confidence can happen at any time and to anyone regardless of their experience level – from beginner to professional.

Fear is my friend. But it wasn't always so. In the summer of 2006, I was bucked off one of my own horses. A horse I had bred, raised, trained and trusted. I had been self-employed as a horse trainer and riding coach for several years at this point. As a horsewoman with over 30 years of experience working with horses, I had come off horses many times before this event. For some reason, this one really shook my confidence and self doubt began creeping in. I would get nervous about getting on any horse. But, I had to get on clients horses. I would get on, but it took a great deal of mental preparation, and if at all possible, I would avoid riding. The fear was getting worse and was often irrational. Fear had become my adversary. If I wasn't able to rebuild my confidence and control my fear, I would have to give up my profession and my passion and look for another way to make a living. I chose to learn how to overcome the fear. And that, really, is the first step for anyone dealing with fear or loss of confidence – making the choice to overcome it.

The information in this book is based on lessons I have learned through my journey to regain my confidence and overcome my fear. The old adage about just getting back on after a fall doesn't always work and sometimes is neither possible nor sensible. I share with you the tools that I have personally used and now teach to my private students and in my workshops.

Overcoming fear and building confidence is primarily a mental battle. You need to take control of your thoughts, change beliefs that no longer serve you and stop your negative self talk – those tapes in your head that are so hard on you. This journey requires self reflection, determination, persistence and support.

I recommend that you set aside quiet, private time where you will be uninterrupted to do the exercises outlined in this book. Some exercises may take more than one session and you may find that answers come to you at unexpected times. I also encourage you to keep a journal to record your thoughts, feelings and insights and as a record of your progress.

You may find, as I did, that as you build or regain your confidence around horses, you also develop more confidence in other areas of your life. I have developed a level of self-confidence that has given me the courage to pursue dreams I once thought were beyond my reach. Okay for someone else but not for me. Conducting the Women, Horses and Fear workshops was the first dream. Writing this book was the next!

It is a journey worth taking as you will become a better, stronger person for it. Our horses need us to be the best we can be – to become the rider our horse deserves.

Anxiety, intimidation, fear; whatever you call it ...

Part 1

THE MENTAL SIDE OF FEAR

"Fear is created not by the world around us, but in the mind, by what we think is going to happen."

~ Elizabeth Gawain

Chapter 1 - You Are Not Alone

You are not the only person who is afraid of horses or has lost confidence riding. Even if you have been around horses all (or most) of your life and have ridden for years, fear or anxiety can destroy your confidence. Joy and fun are replaced with doubt and dread.

You may have developed fear after being injured by a horse or falling off while riding. It may have started after you witnessed somebody else have a riding accident. You may be brand new to the world of horses either because you are starting to ride or someone you care about is a rider. You may not even know the reason behind your fear. Maybe you are returning to riding or being around horses after taking years off to devote to your career or raise your family. Your age, changes in your physical health, increased financial and family responsibilities can all have an unconscious affect on our sense of security and level of risk taking.

"Why aren't we allowed to talk about our fear?" is a question often asked in the Women, Horses and Fear workshops I conduct. As the women share their stories of fear, several common themes emerge – excuses for not riding; the physical symptoms of not being able to breathe, having "jelly legs", and freezing up; feeling frustrated and angry with themselves. But the most startling commonality is the feeling of being alone in their fear. Workshop participants are surprised to find that they were "not the only one" going through this experience.

I believe that fear is not talked about by horse people because of the mindset of traditional horse training and riding. Traditional training techniques require the human to be in control all the time and as much force as is necessary is used to ensure that control. When I was learning to ride, I was often reminded to not show any signs of fear around horses as the horse would sense my fear and then be able to dominate me. I was also taught to never let the horse "win". This method means, of course, that there is a winner and a loser every time a person is with a horse. The relationship between horse and human becomes competitive rather than cooperative. So when I was younger, I would hide any fear by "being tough". It was okay to be tough (or angry) with my horse. It wasn't okay to be afraid. Not the best way to establish a healthy relationship.

For whatever reason, in the horse world we don't feel comfortable talking about or admitting our fear. Instead we find ways to procrastinate or avoid riding - the weather's too windy or too nice; or we just don't have the time as we find other "commitments". And the more we avoid it, the more fear gains a strangle hold on us. Every woman in my workshops had a dream about the way their lives with horses would be. They had a passion about horses and, at one time, horses brought joy into their lives. As the fear grew, their passion and joy were taken away and were replaced by guilt, embarrassment and shame.

To live with a sense of safety and security, we allow ourselves to believe that we are in control. Then something happens to shatter that illusion. The dormant seeds of fear that rest within our psyche take root. With our thoughts, feelings and actions, we feed those seedlings and the vine that is fear takes a stronger hold. Unless a vine is cut back, it eventually covers and destroys whatever it is growing on. And, if the root of the vine – just like the root of your fear – remains intact, the vine will grow back.

The big question in my workshops is, "How do I get over this fear?" We get over our fear in the same way we get control of an over grown vine - by cutting it back bit by bit. It requires time commitment and self-reflection.

You will need to:

1) Analyze & understand the origins of your fear
2) Look at the emotion objectively so you can intellectualize it
3) Develop a plan to counteract it
4) Implement that plan
6) Enlist a support system

Nothing in life is to be feared, it is only to be understood. Now is the time to understand more, so that we may fear less.~ Marie Curie

Know Your Fear

Fear is a perfectly natural and instinctual response that is meant to keep you safe from harm. It can be your protector or your oppressor. As your friend, fear alerts you to potential physical or even emotional danger. It signals you to pay more attention to what you are doing, where you are and what or who is around you. It prepares you physically and mentally to fight or take flight.

Because fear is a perfectly natural, instinctual reaction you cannot completely eliminate it – nor should you want to. But you can learn to decrease and manage its affects on you so that they do not become inappropriately over stimulated and out of control. Don't feel discouraged if your fear doesn't vanish quickly or completely. You may be able to put it into hibernation for awhile but one day it will unexpectedly re-awaken taking you by surprise. However, you will be able to decrease it from a stressful scream to a more manageable whimper.

Fear is a mental battle. We all naturally want safety and security, but they are illusions created in our minds. The true reality is that the potential to be hurt physically or emotionally is always present in all aspects of our lives. We can minimize risks and the potential for getting hurt, but we can never eliminate it totally. Fortunately, most of us do not focus every minute of our conscious thinking in our daily lives on all of the possible dangers that exist. If we did, we simply would not be able to function. You can learn to do the same around horses.

The patterns of behaviour related to your fear have a protective function, but you always pay a price for that protection. Ask yourself – 'what will happen if I change this behaviour – if I am no longer afraid? What will I be able to do? What opportunities will open to me?'

Being aware of the price you pay for all the protection that your fear provides gives you a stronger incentive for taking the continuous action that is necessary to overcome your fear.

Change is uncomfortable. Changing behaviours is challenging. But through the process you will grow and stretch yourself so that you will be able to perform to your highest potential.

Physical Response to Fear

We all feel fear in particular ways in our bodies. When I was feeling fear about riding, I would feel my heart pounding in my chest, butterflies in my stomach and I would often be holding my breath. My neck and shoulders would be tense. I would literally be shaking in my boots.

When fear becomes overwhelming it controls you and negatively impacts your life by interfering with the enjoyment of activities you would like to do. To take back control and manage your fear, it helps to understand what causes those anxious and fearful feelings in the first place.

Experts debate whether fear is initiated by our conscious or unconscious minds. What they do know is that our thoughts, feelings, behaviour and emotions are all linked in a chain reaction. First, your unconscious (subconscious) mind starts asking questions about what you are doing, why you are doing it, if you need to be doing it, and how long you will be doing it for. Then your conscious mind analyses the situation based on the environmental stimuli your senses are receiving– what you are seeing, hearing, smelling or feeling. If you cannot offer a sensible, logical, rational explanation for what is happening around you and your subconscious mind makes a connection to a previous negative experience, a small part of your brain called the hypothalamus starts producing stress hormones (adrenaline, noradrenaline and cortisol) that create the fight or flight response.

How your body responds to fear may not be exactly the same as mine. More than one of my students would cry and become mentally and physically stuck when they were afraid. Another student would get angry and lash out at her horse or shout at me. One student was so anxious about showing that she would be nauseous the night before the competition and not be able to sleep.

Your physical symptoms of fear may include some or all of the following in varying degrees:

- becoming nauseous
- feeling hot or cold;
- getting a headache;
- having a knot in your stomach;
- being unable to eat;
- shortness of breath;
- dry mouth;
- shaking;
- inability to speak;
- inability to think clearly;
- inability to concentrate or focus

Incidentally, your horse experiences similar physical reactions when he or she is stressed or anxious.

These physical symptoms of fear are triggered as soon as the stress hormones are released and each one has a specific purpose:

- Your peripheral vision narrows so that you can focus on an escape route.
- You sweat and feel clammy as blood is drawn away from the skin's surface to important organs.
- You get "goose bumps" as the muscles under your skin contract slightly in preparation for quick action. Your heart pounds as it increases its output and your blood pressure goes up. Your breathing becomes rapid so that more oxygen is transferred to your blood.
- Your spleen releases more red blood cells.
- Non essential systems are inhibited so your digestion slows down and speaking becomes difficult.

That is the technical explanation of how fear works. So, there is really no point in beating yourself up because you experience the symptoms of fear. These physiological, psychological and behavioural responses are perfectly normal. Their purpose is to help you deal with potentially harmful, even life threatening, situations. Everyone who has ever been around horses or ridden for any length of time has felt fear at some time. If they tell you otherwise they are not being honest with you and perhaps not with themselves. Some people may call it a "healthy respect" rather than fear. But it is only common sense to be aware and cautious around a large animal that is physically more powerful than you and has a strong flight instinct.

The exercise on the next page will help you to identify your body's response of fear. The sooner you recognize these physical symptoms the more quickly you can take pro-active actions to diminish their effects before they become overwhelming.

Exercise – Identify Your Body's Fear Response

1. List the physical symptoms that appear when you first begin to feel nervous or fearful:

_____

_____

_____

_____

_____

_____

2. Describe the activity you are doing or your thoughts when you first notice the above symptoms:

_____

_____

_____

_____

_____

_____

3. List the physical symptoms that appear as your anxiety or fear progresses:

_____

_____

_____

_____

_____

_____

"I have learned over the years that when one's mind is made up, this diminishes fear; knowing what must be done does away with fear."

~ Rosa Parks

Types of Fear

Fear is a very basic and primitive mechanism designed to keep you safe from possible danger. All animals including humans have the innate fight, flight, freeze or faint response to fear. While fear is a human instinct, we are, in fact, born with only 2 fears – fear of falling and fear of loud noises. The rest of our fears are learned through our experiences and associations.

Post-traumatic Fear:
Our brains are programmed to remember and recognize potentially dangerous situations in two ways – consciously and unconsciously. All animals have an unconscious "fear memory" located in the lower (primitive) part of the brain called the amygdala where subconscious thought and instinctive behaviour is controlled.

This system is works well for animals living in a predator rich environment who's survival depends on a "run first ask questions later" system. But, it is not a healthy or enjoyable way for any of us to live!

An unconscious fear memory can be created from physical or emotional trauma. If we witness or experience a car accident or a fall from a horse, the amygdala will always remember the trauma and will initiate an unconscious fear response when it recognizes a trigger. For example, consider a person who had a fall when her horse stumbled on a muddy trail at the same time a piece of paper blew in front of them. During that experience, the rider's visual and auditory senses were highly acute and things seemed to happen in slow motion. She remembers every detail vividly – the sound of the wind, the smell of the wet earth, the movement and sound of the leaves on the trees, where the other horses were, where the sun was, etc. A few weeks later, the same person is riding her horse on the trail on a warm, sunny day when the wind picks up a bit. Suddenly, she feels anxious as her heart rate increases, her muscles tense and she freezes. The unconscious fear response was triggered from the amygdala by the sound of the wind which it now sees as a sign of potential danger.

If the rider has had many good experiences of riding on the same trail on warm, breezy days, then the conscious brain may override the fear response. The rider will be able to recognize that there is no danger, relax and enjoy her ride. If the rider does not have that experience, she may lose her confidence about riding on the trails.

The unconscious fear memory will never be erased entirely, but you can override it. You can train the amygdala to replace the freeze response with something less debilitating – even something as simple as taking one step.

General Anxiety:

If you have not had a traumatic experience around horses or while riding, it is still possible for you to lose confidence, feel anxious or be fearful. If you feel that you cannot control situations or the results of your actions or choices, you may imagine the worst case scenario. In small doses this is called worrying. But, when worrying becomes a habit it can turn into general anxiety which can be debilitating.

Anxiety is a fear caused by negative future thinking … the "what if" syndrome. People can be very creative when thinking about all the potential catastrophes that can happen around a horse. Even though the potential danger is only in your mind and is being caused by your own thoughts, your body still responds as if the danger were real and imminent.

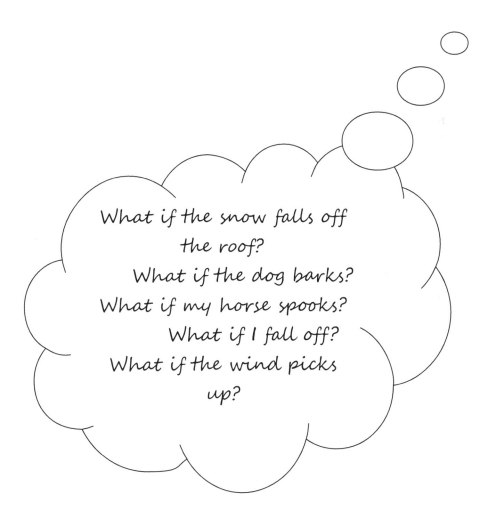

What if the snow falls off the roof?
What if the dog barks?
What if my horse spooks?
What if I fall off?
What if the wind picks up?

Fear caused by anxiety is more common in adults than in children. And there are many reasons for that. You may have noticed changes in your body cause you to:

- be less supple and have stiffer joints;
- be less able to "bounce";
- be more aware of your physical vulnerability;
- feel injuries (even minor ones) more; and,
- need longer to recover from injuries.

In addition to the physical aspects, adults have a lot more on our minds than children do. You may:

- have many competing demands on your time, energy and finances;
- be the main care giver for children or elderly parents;
- be an important part of or the sole provider to the family income;
- worry more about what others think about you;
- have very high expectations of yourself and your results.

That is a lot of "stuff" running around in your brain. These thoughts keep you focused on the future and possible negative outcomes instead of being in the present moment and aware of what is really happening.

Your anxiety could be a reflection of other things that are going on in your life. If you are generally a nervous, anxious person who experiences similar feelings of stress or fear at work, home or socially, you are not likely to be confident or calm in your horse related activities. One of my students struggled with a lack of confidence that set back her riding ability a great deal. Around the same time, she was dealing with her elderly mother's illness and then her death. She was the executor of her mother's will and there was some animosity from her siblings. A few months later, this same client's sister suffered a heart attack. With all that stress in her life, it is no wonder she was struggling with her riding. However, this woman was very motivated to ride and was willing to take the steps necessary to rebuild her confidence. Her riding lessons became less about physical skills and more about the mental and physical awareness. She developed the ability to stay in the moment, breathe and release tension. These are all good skills that she could apply in her everyday life as well as with her horse.

If you have stressful issues in other parts of your life, seeking help to deal with them may help to decrease the stress associated with your horse related activities.

The exercise on the next page will help you define and clarify your fear.

Exercise – Understand Your Fear

Define & describe the type of fear you have:

_____

_____

_____

What is your earliest memory of having this fear?

_____

_____

_____

What kind of physical reactions do you have to this fear?

_____

_____

_____

What are some of the things this fear keeps you from doing or takes the enjoyment out of doing?

_____

_____

_____

How might your life change if you were able to overcome the fear?

_____

_____

_____

Does this fear overlap into other areas of your life? If so, how and what are they?

_____

_____

_____

"Courage is not the absence of fear, but rather the judgment that something else is more important than fear."

~ Ambrose Redmoon

Developing Courage

You may not feel very courageous right now, but let me assure you that whenever you are facing your fears, you are acting with courage. Courage is all in your head. It is defined as the emotional and mental ability to face and deal with difficult, dangerous and challenging situations. It is the psychological ability that helps you meet life's challenges head on. No one is born courageous. Courage is developed through the practice of facing your fear. The more you practice, the more courageous you become. As Mark Twain said, *"Courage is not the absence of fear. It is acting in spite of it."*

You can develop more courage by having real conviction about what it is that you want to do and why you want to do it. Being clear about why you want to do whatever it is you are fearful of gives you a sense of purpose. With a sense of purpose you will have more motivation to do the work you need to do to overcome your fears. Instead of focusing on the possible negative outcomes of your activities, you will be able to focus more on the positive results.

Sometimes, your sense of purpose has changed without you consciously realizing it. For example, some people get into riding because it is an activity that they can share with friends or family. When one of my friends (I'll call her "Sandra") began riding as an adult, she took dressage lessons with her daughter. The daughter took her riding very seriously. She

17

competed on the Young Riders' team. When the daughter left home for university and then subsequently went to Europe as a working student for a couple of high level riders, Sandra's motivation for riding changed. She semi-retired the older mare she had ridden for several years and bought a young horse. She lost her confidence, sold the young horse and gave up riding for a while. Sandra kept her older mare at a friend's private farm. Her friend is an avid rider who enjoys trail riding as well as low level competition. The friend encouraged Sandra to go for trail rides with her on her old mare. Sandra discovered that she really enjoyed trail riding and so did her old mare. With a renewed sense of purpose focused on pleasure riding rather than dressage, she regained her confidence and her passion for riding.

In a slightly different situation, another friend also started riding when her young daughter began taking lessons. In this case, it was the daughter who lost her confidence and interest in riding. She was only riding because she did not want to disappoint her mother. After having an honest discussion about the situation, they agreed that the daughter should stop riding and focus on other activities. The mother in this story continues to enjoy riding recreationally and as a social activity.

Another friend lost her passion for not only riding but for teaching riding lessons. For a while, she continued to ride despite feeling uncomfortable and not really enjoying it. It took some courage for her to admit to herself, her family, friends and clients that she did not really want to ride. Her real passion was for working with horses from the ground. She now enjoys teaching other women the magic of connecting with horses in this way.

All three of these situations illustrate the importance of how being clear on your sense of purpose – the reasons for doing what you do – can help you develop courage and eventually overcome your fear. If your dreams or priorities have changed or you are riding only to please someone else, your fear may really be providing an excuse for you to not participate. Subconsciously, you may have no real desire to eliminate the fear. You might need to find the courage to admit that you actually do not want to ride or be involved with horses. You might need to change the type of riding you do. For example, deciding that showing is not really for you and choosing to ride only for pleasure (or vice versa). You might decide that you really enjoy working with horses from the ground the most and choose to give up riding all together.

The following exercise will help you clarify your purpose for overcoming your fears and building your confidence in your horse related activities.

"Worry is a thin stream of fear trickling through the mind. If encouraged, it cuts a channel into which all other thoughts are drained."
~ Arthur Somers Roche

Exercise ~ Define Your Purpose for Overcoming Your Fear

Answering the following questions will help you to define your purpose:

Why is overcoming this fear important?

I want to learn how to jump a Roanie + need to develop confidence. I the young TB overall.

Who is it important to? Why?

Me-

Is it because of your own passion and desire or to please someone else?

No

Define your personal purpose for overcoming your fear of horses and/or riding.

to learn something new each day - go beyond my comfort level.

"We don't see things as they are; we see them as we are."

~ Anais Nin

Chapter 2 - Developing Awareness

Self Awareness

Horses are highly aware creatures that can read us through the most subtle cues given by our bodies and breathing. Most humans, however, tend to be disconnected from themselves physically and mentally. Not understanding your own behaviours and feelings is like giving over control of yourself to a stranger. You cannot change what you are not aware of.

Self awareness means being present and consciously clear about who you are, what you want, and what you are doing. It is empowering to be actively aware and in control of your physical, mental and emotional states. If you are not, you get caught up in your own internal dramas with your unconscious thoughts and beliefs determining your feelings and behaviour.

Ask yourself if your mind is your best friend or your worst enemy. If you are not in control of your thoughts, then your thoughts control you. You become trapped in an unending loop of old thoughts and beliefs that no longer benefit you. You remain stuck in the same unconscious patterns that can stop you from moving forward and sabotage your best intentions.

When you are not fully present and aware, you go through life on auto-pilot living by habit and reacting unconsciously. With self awareness, you live consciously in the present moment with intention, focus and purpose. You become proactive rather than reactive. You can only become self aware when you stop and pay attention to your thoughts, feelings (physical and mental), emotions and behaviours. Then you can become aware of the beliefs that sabotage your best intentions and discover the root causes of your blocks, negativity, fears, emotions and pain.

Write It Down

Keeping a journal is a good way to develop self awareness through your mind, body and heart. There are many ways to journal but the basic idea is to capture and process your thoughts and feelings on paper or your computer.

Journaling is not simply writing down what you did each day. Your journal is a safe place to release your thoughts and feelings without fear of judgment. It is private and for your eyes only. You can journal at any time, but it works best when you set aside a specific time of day and place where you will be undisturbed. For me, journaling in the mornings before starting my day works best. Write without censoring yourself. Don't worry about spelling, punctuation or grammar. Just let your thoughts flow and write them down as quickly as you can. Let it be messy.

When I first started keeping a journal, I often found it difficult to commit my thoughts to paper. My mind would be frantic with thoughts until I had pen and paper ready and then my mind just seemed to lock. I would be sitting staring at the blank page wondering what in the world I was doing. I learned about the practise of writing anything down just to get your hand moving across the page (or keyboard) until you have filled 3 pages or have written for 10 minutes. I had many pages filled with "blah, blah, blah – this is stupid – blah, blah, blah – my head is empty". But, then all of a sudden a real thought or idea would slip through and that would get written on the page without censoring. As I stayed committed to writing in my journal every morning the process become easier and the thoughts flowed more clearly.

Journaling can be a beneficial tool even if you only use it occasionally. But, I encourage you to make the commitment to write in your journal every day at the same time of day, in the same location and for a certain length of time. Try it for a week – just 7 days – and see what happens. When you use it regularly and with purpose, journaling has an astounding power to help you consciously connect with your subconscious mind. It is your subconscious mind that holds your thought patterns and limiting beliefs. However, it also holds your inner strength, your intuition and your potential. By the daily practice of journaling you can open up to insights, wisdom and creativity that you didn't know were inside you.

Breathe with Calm Focused Breath

I teach this technique to all of my students – and I use it myself. When you're stressed, anxious, or fearful, you breathe with short, shallow breaths, without any rhythm, and often even hold your breath. This keeps those stress hormones (adrenaline and cortisol) going through your body. This is what makes you feel nauseous, shake and sweat. Your heart pounds and your body tenses. Your head aches. You go "fetal" – tipping forward in the saddle.

None of these symptoms of stress are fun – for you or for your horse. Horses are incredibly sensitive to the body language and energy of the people around them. They even mirror your breathing. This is why your stress and tension can affect how your horse feels. As soon as you recognize the first symptom of fear, changing your breathing is the fastest way to help you to feel more calm and confident.

Try this breathing exercise:

- Sit in a chair with your feet flat on the ground, your back straight and your chest open. Let your hands rest gently on your lap.

- Breathe in through your nose and out through your mouth

- Put one hand on your belly (at your navel) and the other hand on your chest

- Focus on your breath

- Count to 5 slowly as you inhale and feel your belly expand and then your chest lift slightly

- Hold your breath for a count of 3

- Exhale slowly for a count of 5. Feel your chest drop and your belly deflate moving back towards your spine.

- Your heart may pump a bit more to start with as it adjusts to the new way you are breathing. It will soon pass and you will feel more calm and relaxed.

- Repeat several more times - inhaling for a count of 5, holding for 3, exhaling for a count of 5 – feeling the movement your belly out as in inhale and in as you exhale.

- Practice this new way of breathing as often as you can throughout your day. Anytime you feel stressed or anxious, take a few slow, CALM FOCUSED BREATHS and notice how quickly you calm down.

- The more you practice, the more natural it will feel.

This way of breathing allows your mind to slow down and relax. When you are in a relaxed state you're better able to see things as they really are because you're not experiencing the cluttered thinking caused by your emotions._ With practice, you'll be able to calm your mind using your calm focused breathing exercise any time. This practice allows you to respond to stressful events with a level head, and you'll find that your emotions are less in control of you. The next time you feel anxiety or fear creeping into your mind, remember that you have a choice. You can react from your emotions and complicate the situation or you can respond in a way that encourages you and your horse to feel more calm and confident.

With calm focused breathing, and the relaxation it brings, you're always only a few short minutes away from the stress relief you crave. Instead of reacting negatively when you feel anxious or afraid, you'll look for solutions and feel more confident. The choice is always yours.

In the meantime, take a few minutes today to practice your calm focused breath, clear your mind of its worries, and relax. Do the same tomorrow and the next day. Like physical exercise, the benefits of this breathing exercise are accumulative. The more you practice, the more benefits you'll receive and the better you'll become at staying calm and building your confidence.

Body Focus

Poor posture, stress, fear and even cold temperatures can be the cause of stiffness, tension and imbalance in your body. Being out of balance also causes tension in the body which contributes to feeling insecure and fearful. It can be a vicious circle. Of course, your horse responds to what he sees and feels from your body. Any tension, stiffness and imbalance he feels from you will affect his confidence as well as his ability to perform well.

We all have patterns of tension in certain places in our bodies. These are the places that our mental stress goes as well as tension caused from poor posture, previous injuries or just lack of proper exercise and stretching. We are often not even be aware of the pattern or where we hold the tension. Many adults carry their stress in their necks and shoulders. Others carry it in their hips or even in their jaws. Tension causes the muscle to contract. If the tension accumulates, the contracted muscle can pull on the bones tugging them out of alignment and creating compensation patterns. Some muscles are overused to compensate for the under use of the compromised muscle. The muscles can't function as they should sometimes resulting in cramps, strain and pain.

By paying attention, you can identify where you commonly hold your tension and learn how to release it. Practise these exercises first on the ground and then on your horse. On the ground stand with your feet hip width apart. Let your shoulders drop away from your ears and hang down your rib cage. Let your pelvis rest on your legs. Feel the connection of your feet to the ground. Notice whether your weight is over your toes, over your heels or in the middle of your feet. Gently and slowly shift your weight forwards, to centre, backwards and back to centre. Notice how your body feels in each of these positions.

Gently lengthen your spine and torso by opening your chest and abdomen. With every inhale, visualize the space between your ribs opening and your spine lengthening. Keep your body relaxed by working with your breath and avoiding aggressive muscular effort.

Once you are standing grounded over your feet, scan your body for the areas where you are holding tension. Start at the top of your head and work your way down through your face, neck, shoulders, upper, middle & lower back, arms (focus on one at a time) – elbows, wrists, fingers; hips, legs (focus on one at a time) – thighs, knees, calves, ankles, toes. When you find an area where you are holding tension, stop and breathe deeply (calm focused breath) into that area until you feel the muscles relax. Only after you have released the tension in that area continue your body scan.

If you can't release the tension by breathing then try tensing the area more, holding it for about 5 seconds and then releasing it. For example, if your neck and shoulders are tense, scrunch your shoulders up towards your ears. Hold that position for 5 seconds and then release your shoulders down as far away from your ears as you comfortably can.

Try the same exercises when you are sitting on your horse. Find the same alignment in your body as you had when standing on the ground – ears over shoulders over hips over heels. Feel your rib cage opening and your spine lengthening as you ground yourself over your seat bones and legs. Feel your seat bones now the same way you felt your feet when you did this as a standing exercise. Slowly and gently shift your weight slightly forwards, then centre, then slightly backwards and finally back to centre.

Be patient and gentle with yourself and your body. If you have habitually been holding tension in an area for a long period of time you will not completely fix it immediately. Change will not come by forcing it. Make stretching a regular part of your daily routine. Do a body scan to check for tension throughout the day whether you are driving, working at your desk or in the barn, or walking. You may also find that taking a yoga or tai chi class is a great way to develop more awareness for your body as you learn how to release stress and tension.

Eye Focus

Fear causes your vision to become less focused and to shut down. You get tunnel vision as your peripheral vision actually becomes more narrow.

Try this exercise. Place a hard focus on a particular target. Notice what you can see and how you feel. Now, soften and unfocus your eyes. Take in as many details as possible – people, colours, movements, reactions. Consciously think about each detail. Notice how much more you see and how you feel.

Mental Awareness

Fear is not only created by very real, tangible things – things you can touch, hear, and see – but also by things created by your mind, imagination and beliefs. It all starts with your thoughts. Your thoughts set the direction of your feelings.

Your feelings affect your action or inaction. And that all affects how you feel physically.

You Are What You Think About

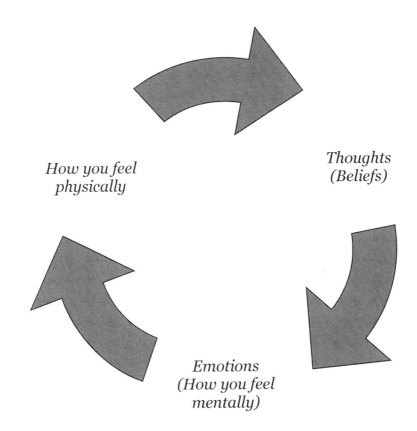

*Thoughts
(Beliefs)*

*How you feel
physically*

*Emotions
(How you feel
mentally)*

Self Talk and Beliefs

Our biggest critic lives inside our own heads. It's that little voice that carries on a never ending dialogue with you and gives a running commentary about everything you do, every decision you make and everything you want to do. It is there when you are stressed and even when you have simple daily concerns. It has an opinion about everything

Your self talk comes from your own belief system. Held in your subconscious, these beliefs came from experiences you had or things you heard from parents, teachers or other significant figures from your childhood. They become incorporated into your personality as limiting beliefs that control your life even they are not true. They affect the way you see yourself and the world. We see things not as they are but as we are.

When you try to do something that goes against your existing beliefs, your inner critic speaks up loudly and shuts you down. Limiting beliefs are absolutes and often irrational. How many of these limiting thoughts do you recognize?

- I'm not as good as I used to be.
- I'm too old to do this
- I just know something will go wrong
- I won't try anything new because I won't be good at it right away
- I'm not as good as everyone else or everyone else is better than me.
- If I did it well it must have been a fluke.

- If I can't do it perfectly or be the best at it, I won't do it.
- I'm not good or smart enough
- I just can't do it.
- I never finish anything
- I never succeed or win at anything
- I can't change

When your self talk focuses on the negative, a small problem can become blown out of all proportion as you focus on all the things that could go wrong and you play the "what if" game. This focus on the outcome of your actions moves your awareness out of the present and into the future. Your confidence decreases as your stress and anxiety increase.

Although you cannot get rid of your inner voice, you can learn how to control your mind so that it becomes your friend rather your enemy. In order to change limiting beliefs into empowering ones, you must pay attention to your thoughts and rephrase negative statements into positive ones. As self-help guru, Dr. Wayne Dyer says, "You'll see it when you believe it."

The first step is to become aware of what your inner voice is saying. Identify the positive as well as the negative thoughts. Then you can make a conscious effort to purposely include more positive, beneficial thoughts. One way to become more aware of your self talk is to consciously pay attention to your thoughts when you are in a stressful situation. Write your thoughts down in your journal as they come up without censoring or stopping them. Afterwards, review them and ask whether each thought is rational or irrational. Consider how each thought makes you feel. Decide if the thought is beneficial or harmful to your self confidence and self esteem.

Thought stopping is an effective technique that replaces negative thoughts with positive ones. As soon as you are aware of a negative thought stop it by simply saying "stop it" to yourself or visualizing a large red "X" or stop sign. Then replace the negative thought with a positive one. Thought stopping is easier if you plant the positive thoughts before your self talk spirals downwards. Here are some examples to get you started:

Negative Thought	Positive Thought
I'm not as good as I used to be	I enjoy the activity and socializing with my friends
I did it well but it was only a fluke.	I did it well once, I can do it again.
I just know something will go wrong	Nothing will go wrong. I have the skills to cope.
I can't do it perfectly.	I can learn one step at a time and improve over time.

Visualization

Another helpful technique is to change the pictures you see in your mind. Visualization is a strong and proven technique used successfully by professional and world class amateur athletes to improve their skills and confidence. Your mind does not know the difference between a real and an imagined event. If you keep replaying in your mind the mistakes you have made or situations that you imagine might happen, your mind believes you. If you change your mental video tape from the possible catastrophic outcome to seeing the positive outcome you desire, your mind believes that as well.

You can't change what happened in the past, but you can use what happened to influence the future. Everyone – even professional riders – makes mistakes and has bad rides. So, instead of beating yourself up or scaring yourself by replaying the video in your mind of what went wrong, do what the high performing riders do. They study videos of their rides to see where they can make improvements. Then they mentally rehearse a better outcome for the next time. When you can envision another way to deal with a situation then you prepare yourself to know what to do (and what not to do) in a similar situation.

Thoughts and words are powerful whether you are listening to your own self talk or to the words, thoughts and beliefs of others. Pay attention to the people you spend time with on a regular basis. Are you hanging out with negative people who spend time gossiping, judging others, draining your energy and making you feel bad about yourself? You need to surround yourself with people who will offer you support and encouragement on your journey; people who will pick you up when you falter; people who can inspire and motivate you to be the best you can be. These are the people who should be your Support Team.

Be compassionate with yourself. Would you let someone speak to your best friend or child the same way you talk to yourself? Give yourself the same consideration and support. You need to build yourself up rather than tear yourself down.

Look for solutions instead of focusing on problems. Be aware of your weaknesses so you know what you need to work on to improve. But focus on your strengths and what you do well and build on those. Every time you spend time with your horse, have a lesson or compete in a show:

- find at least one positive aspect of your experience;
- acknowledge what you need to work on rather than what you "messed up";
- avoid comparing yourself to anyone else;

- compete only with yourself and no one else;
- write this all down in your journal.

It's time to stop being so hard on yourself and terrorizing yourself. Become your own cheerleader! You do have the ability to change your mind. Whether it is through journaling, what you say to yourself or the pictures you play in your mind – or a combination of all three – choose to use your imagination for good rather than evil. Create a positive outcome in your mind first and you will see the results in your reality.

The exercise on the next page will help you develop your mental awareness.

Exercise – Develop Mental Awareness

Write down your answers to the following questions. Don't edit them as you write or worry about anyone else seeing this. It is for your eyes only.

1. Write down all the thoughts you have been telling yourself about your riding ability or comfort level around horses, how good you are and how good your horse is.

decent rider, have alot to learn
comfortable around horses but always
aware of their unpredictability → dangerous

2. Write about your current (or most recent) riding or horse related experiences. How much fun have you had? How well has your horse been going or behaving? Where have you been riding or spending time with horses?

Having fun = both Ronnie + Capp
Ronnie is improving = training & behavior

Is there a link between your current pattern of thought and your present experiences? This is not a coincidence. Your experience (reality) is a perfect reflection of your thoughts (perception).

3. Identify the negative thoughts or statements you say to yourself.

_____

_____

_____

_____

_____

_____

4. List positive, beneficial statements you can use to replace your negative, harmful thoughts. Ensure they are meaningful to you personally.

_____

_____

_____

_____

_____

5. How do you picture the outcome of your experience with riding or being with horses?

_____

_____

_____

_____

_____

_____

6. Use your imagination to visualize a positive outcome. Describe it in detail.

_____

_____

_____

_____

_____

_____

7. Write down what you would say to a child or your best friend if they were feeling anxious or scared in a similar situation.

_____

_____

_____

_____

_____

_____

_____

"People are never more insecure than when they become obsessed with their fears at the expense of their dreams."

~ *Norman Cousins*

Chapter 3 - Stress and Recovery

Fear is stressful and exhausting. It takes mental and physical energy to manage your fear. But the stress eats up your energy. It is a vicious circle. While you are feeling fearful, you are stressed and using up the energy you need to manage your fear.

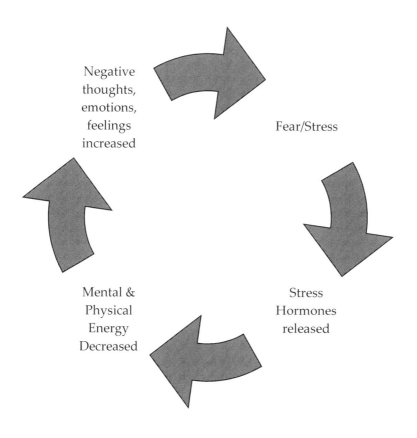

Negative thoughts, emotions, feelings increased

Fear/Stress

Stress Hormones released

Mental & Physical Energy Decreased

Stress is cumulative. Stress coming from other areas of your life not related to horses and riding can negatively affect your horse and riding time. You need to identify the stressors in your life and find ways to reduce their negative impact on you. Simply stated, you will not have the energy you need to work through your fear while you are stressed out. Stress can be caused by situations at home and at work, your life responsibilities or your daily routine. Stress is a very individual phenomenon. What you find to be stressful may not bother someone else and vice versa.

4 Steps For Coping And Recovery

There are four steps you can take in the short term to help you cope with and recover from stress both in your daily life and your horse related activities. Learn to **choose, avoid, alter** and **accept**.

1. **Choose** your battles. Be picky about the situations and people you allow to excite or upset you, use up your time and energy, or endanger a relationship. As much as possible, avoid spending time with negative people. For those you can't avoid being around (for example, work colleagues or family members), develop ways to minimize their affect on you. Don't allow their 'drama' to become your drama.

2. **Avoid** perfectionism and comparing yourself to others. Perfectionism is unrealistic, frustrating and unattainable. Unrealistic expectations are characterized by the words such as "should," "if only," and "ought" in your self-talk. (eg. I should be able to do that. I should be doing better.) Focus on and experience your own journey and let others do the same. We are all 'perfectly imperfect' works in progress.

3. **Alter** your attitude and self-talk. Whatever you are saying, you are always listening. Change your negative self-talk into positive. Change your perspective from seeing your experiences not as successes and failures, but as lessons. Lighten up! Develop a strong sense of humour. Recognize and focus on your talents more than on your limitations. It is your talents and strengths that make you the unique and special individual that you are.

4. **Accept** what you cannot change. There are situations that are out of your control that you cannot change. You cannot change anyone other than yourself. Accept it. See yourself, others and situations as they are without adding any drama and you can deal with them more effectively.

To cope with and recover from stress in the long term, you need to break the cycle of

Fear/Stress $\rightarrow$ Stress Hormones $\rightarrow$ Energy Drain $\rightarrow$ Negative Feelings.

You need to literally give yourself a break. The only way to recover your energy is to make the time to do activities that help you relax and rejuvenate. After all, you are no good to yourself or anybody else when your cup is empty. So, go ahead and give yourself permission to take the time - that means you have to make the time - for yourself.

Your break doesn't have to be a week's vacation or a day at the spa – although either of those options are great. In reality, you might legitimately not be able to take that amount of time right now. So here is a suggestion for a simple way to start making yourself feel better and more positive. It only takes a few minutes at the end of the day. All you need is a notebook or piece of paper and a pen or your computer.

Start keeping these two lists:

1. **Success List** – In a notepad, on a piece of paper or on a computer file make a list at the end of every day of what you did that helped you move – even a little bit – towards your goal. These are things you got done that were for you; that moved you forward even tiny wee bit. This is a short list that includes things like – scheduled a riding lesson; ordered that training DVD; picked up the entries for the show. They may be little things, but they are moving you forward.

   These are the little steps you need to take – and keep taking - to reach your goals. Each one is a sign that you are succeeding by taking action. On the days when you don't feel like you are making any progress, you can look back at this list and see all the little steps you have taken that are moving your forward.

2. **Feel Good List** – Keep this list in a separate section of your notepad, on a different piece of paper or on another computer file. Every time something happens that makes you feel good about being with or riding your horse, write it down. Capture the emotion. Things like – "my horse nickered when I came in the barn today. It made me feel all warm and fuzzy"; "my coach complemented my position today. I felt awesome"; "I picked up Sunshine's feet today. Woo hoo!"

   Good things happen to you a lot. But our brains are programmed to focus on the negative. Update this list every day and then refer back to it whenever you are feeling down. Each little positive step will be a reminder that you are making progress. Remember that progress often happens in baby steps.

Taking a few minutes at the end of each day to add to these two lists will help you feel better about yourself and the progress you are making.

Make time in your schedule for regular opportunities for relaxation and rejuvenation. What works for you is as individual as the causes of fear and stress. It is important for you to understand and acknowledge your own individual needs. There is no one "correct" way to relax and recover. While one person may need active social interaction (e.g. a girls night out), another may need quiet, alone time (e.g. a walk in the woods).

I am physically active most days and also carry the stress of feeling responsible for the safety of my clients (human and equine). I find the stretching and meditation of a yoga class helps me feel rejuvenated, refreshed and relaxed. A good friend who has a stressful office job found that she didn't receive the same benefits from yoga. So, she signed up for a boxing fitness class and loved it. It really pumped her up – mentally as well as physically. One client finds her rejuvenation through running while another finds it through meditation and another finds it spending time with her grandchildren.

Consider the following suggestions for relaxing and rejuvenating. Some can be done in a few minutes throughout your day to day activities. Others require setting aside an hour or more. Set aside some "me" time every day. I like to get up at least a half hour before everyone else to enjoy some quiet reading time over my first cup of coffee of the day. Try out a few of these ideas and find the ones that work best for you.

Practices for De-Stressing

Whatever activity you choose, remember to have compassion for yourself and accept yourself unconditionally. You are perfectly imperfect.

Make a space just for you – your personal quiet, relaxation space – and let others know that you are not to be disturbed when you are there. Get up half an hour before your family or go to bed half an hour later than them, if necessary.

On the next two pages there are lists of suggested Mental and Physical practices that can help you de-stress. Try out as many as you can and make a habit of the ones that work best for you.

"Stress is not what happens to us. It's our response to what happens. And response is something we can choose."

~ Maureen Killoran

Mental Practices

- Choose a healthy, positive attitude.
- Replace "I should" with "I choose".
- Choose an appropriate level of emotional involvement. Avoid taking on other people's drama.
- Say "no" when asked to do something you really don't want to do.
- Do one thing at a time. Focus on it. Do it slowly and with clarity of intent.
- Avoid seeking approval from others.
- Avoid shop talk outside of work.
- Avoid complaining and gossiping
- Prioritize your activities. Do what's most important to you first.
- You can change no one's behaviour except your own.
- Let go of unrealistic expectations of yourself and others.
- Give and accept support from others.
- Eliminate guilt and worry about the past. You cannot change it.
- Spend more time remembering happy times.
- Simplify your life. Eliminate the trivial and unnecessary.
- Make peace and move on.
- Play and laugh often. Laughter releases endorphins, chemicals in the brain that restore calm.
- Seek harmony in life. Enjoy nature, nurturing, music, children
- Become a better listener.
- Respect yourself. Only talk positively about and to yourself.
- Read a good book or a trashy novel
- Practice using prayer or meditation
- Keep a gratitude journal and write in it every evening.
- Keep a journal to write your worries, your feelings and your dreams.
- Have fun

Physical Practices

- Indulge yourself with a bubble bath and soothing music
- Treat yourself to a special beverage
- Go for a short walk or run without interruptions or distractions
- Get a professional therapeutic massage or spa treatment
- Take a yoga class or practice at home with a DVD
- Take slow, deep breaths throughout the day.
- Get enough rest every day – 6 to 8 hours of uninterrupted sleep
- Find ways to exercise daily - take the stairs; park at the far end of the lot, get off the bus one block before your destination
- Eat a healthy, balanced your diet – increase fruits and vegetables, reduce caffeine, sugar and fast foods

Use the exercise on the next page to help you identify the stressors in your life and the methods of recovery that work best for you. Then create a plan for your "me" time.

Exercise – Relax and Recovery Plan

1. Identify the stressors in your life. Stress can be caused by situations or people at home and at work, your life responsibilities or your daily routine.

_____

_____

_____

_____

_____

_____

_____

2. Methods of recovery can include personal quiet time, meditation/prayer, exercise, time with friends, or rest. Identify the recovery methods that work best for you:

_____

_____

_____

_____

_____

_____

_____

3. Plan time for your relax and recovery sessions. For example, setting aside 15 or 20 minutes of daily quiet "me" time to write in your journal can make a significant difference to your stress level. Scheduling a regular adult only evening out with your significant other or close friends can bring some fun back into your life. Create a plan for when you will participate in the relax and recover options that work best for you :

Relax & Recover Activity (eg. Journal)	When –Daily, Weekly or Monthly			Time
	D	W	M	

The purpose of life, after all, is to live it, to taste experience to the utmost, to reach out eagerly and without fear for new er and richer experiences.

"

~ *Eleanor Roosevelt*

Chapter 4 - Comfort Zone

Fear Arousal Scale

Everything you are confident and comfortable doing is within your comfort zone. It is at the low end of your fear arousal scale and is where you feel very comfortable. On a scale of 1 to 10, the comfort zone is from 1 to 4. You are not learning anything new, growing or stretching yourself. This is the zone you want to come back to when you get too stressed or need to regroup.

You know you are leaving your comfort zone and entering the Learning Zone as soon as you begin to feel the minor physical symptoms of anxiety or fear. This zone is from about 5 to 7 on the fear arousal scale and it is where you need to go if you want to learn anything new. You may feel a bit anxious, but you are still interested in what you are doing and able to focus mentally.

When you go too far out of your comfort zone – above 7 on the fear arousal scale – you have entered the Anxiety Zone. You feel overwhelmed which can result in you shutting down mentally and physically. It can escalate into full blown panic. Your body and mind start to shut down as you freeze up, stop hearing, stop seeing and stop taking in external information. If you reach this point, you need to immediately stop what you are doing and take it back to your learning or comfort zone. If you escalate to a 10 on the fear arousal scale, you will be in flat out panic mode.

Fear Arousal Scale

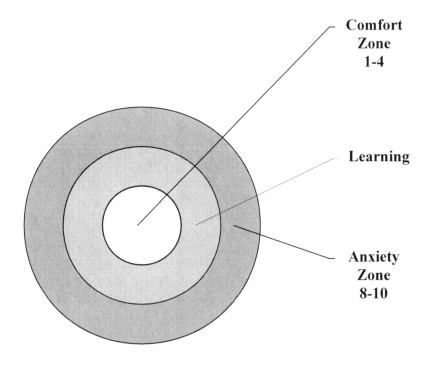

Comfort
Zone
1-4

Learning

Anxiety
Zone
8-10

Marnie came to me for help after she had been trampled by her own horse. He had spooked while she was in the paddock with him and in his panic, had run over top of her. Physically, she was bruised and sore. Mentally, she lost all trust for her horse. In fact, she was afraid to be near any horse on the ground and was terrified if she had to go into a paddock with horses. Since she kept her own horses at home, this situation was causing a great deal of difficulty for her to be able to care for her own horses. Her own safety was compromised because her anxiety affected her horses and made her less able to deal well with day to day chores. When I began working with Marnie, her Comfort Zone was having a fence between herself and the horse.

I worked with Marnie to teach her how to interpret her horse's body language and understand his fears. During our sessions together, Marnie was able to go into the paddock with me without panicking. This was her Learning Zone. If I asked her to go in to the paddock by herself, she could easily move into panic mode. Because Marnie and I discussed her physical symptoms of fear, she could let me know (and usually I could see) when she was becoming too anxious and moving out of her Learning Zone. Then we could take a step back to allow her to calm down before proceeding further.

As Marnie's ability to read and understand her horse's behaviour increased, her Comfort Zone expanded and so did her Learning Zone. As a result, her Anxiety Zone became smaller. Eventually, Marnie was able to comfortably, confidently and safely handle and feed her horses again. She could also enjoy being with her horses again - haltering, grooming, leading and even lunging them safely and confidently. At first, she felt mild discomfort with each activity, but with consistent practice and successful interactions, these feelings went away completely.

When you can identify your own personal fear arousal levels on the scale of 1 to 10, you will be able to use it for yourself and share it with your riding coach. Being clear about your personal fear arousal scale means you will know and can let your instructor know where you are on that scale at any given time.

Take the pressure off yourself by knowing and accepting exactly where your comfort zone and abilities are right now. You can do this by no longer telling yourself or listening to anyone else who tries to tell you what you "should" be able to do. Accepting yourself does not mean that you don't work towards improving and growing. It simply means taking the pressure off yourself by releasing expectations. (You can do the same for your horse.)

The following exercise will help you identify your fear arousal scale – Comfort Zone, Learning Zone and Anxiety Zone.

Exercise – Identify Your Personal Fear Arousal Scale

1. Identify where your comfort zone currently is. This is Level 1-4 on your personal fear arousal scale. What activities are you confident and comfortable doing where you have absolutely no anxiety or discomfort?

_____

_____

_____

_____

_____

2. Your comfort zone ends the exact moment you feel the first symptoms of fear. Identify the precise moment you leave your comfort zone. This Level 5-7 on your personal fear arousal scale. You feel a bit anxious, but are excited and still able to think logically. This is your Learning Zone.

_____

_____

_____

_____

_____

3. Describe the initial physical symptoms (body response) that happen as soon as you leave your comfort zone and move to the learning zone.

_____

_____

_____

_____

_____

4. Describe the thoughts and self talk that happen as soon as you leave your comfort zone and enter your learning zone.

_____

_____

_____

_____

_____

_____

_____

_____

5. Identify your physical and mental symptoms when you leave your Learning Zone and start to become overwhelmed. This is Level 8-10 on your personal fear arousal scale. As soon as you move into this zone, it is time for you to take your activities back down to your Learning or Comfort Zone level to relax and recover.

_____

_____

_____

_____

_____

_____

_____

_____

"We cannot become what we want to be by
remaining what we are."
~ Max DePree

Expand Your Comfort Zone

You feel safe in your Comfort Zone, but staying there for too long leads to feelings of stagnation. Moving from your Comfort Zone to your Learning Zone requires taking small risks – just enough to feel a little bit unsure perhaps even excited without overwhelming you.

Make a plan to slowly but steadily expand your comfort zone with small challenges. Keep an open time line and do not let anyone else decide when you are ready for a challenge. Take baby steps by setting small, short-term goals for improvement that require you to stretch into the Learning Zone without becoming overwhelmed.

It is normal to feel some amount of discomfort as you leave your comfort zone. If you don't, then you are not stretching yourself enough. However, if you start to feel overwhelmed, go back to doing something within your comfort zone until you are no longer feeling anxious. Then start again. The idea is to manage a small amount of discomfort while staying calm and focused. Always end the session on a positive note for both yourself and your horse. Remember to find something positive from the session and write it in your journal.

To help keeping you move in the direction of your goals and dreams, your plan may also include one or more of the following:

- taking regular riding lessons with a supportive riding instructor,
- having sessions with a sports psychologist or psychotherapist experienced with equestrian issues , or
- creating your own Support Team.

Your Support Team is one or more people who you trust and who will support you on your journey. They will give you a gentle push when needed without making you feel bad about yourself. They will boost you up when you feel low. They have your back.

Your beliefs play a large role in keeping you in your comfort zone. These include your beliefs about yourself, your horse, your instructor, etc. Remember that most of your beliefs were established unconsciously and many were ingrained during your childhood. To expand your comfort zone you need to analyze your beliefs and change the ones that are limiting and no longer serving you. When you recognize a belief ask if it is valid and beneficial to you now. If it is not, replace it with an empowering belief. For example, a common limiting belief that many people have is "I am not good enough". Question it by asking "what am I good at?" or "what would it look like if I was good enough?" Then create a new, empowering belief based on your answers to those questions. Keep your mind open to new possibilities.

Always accept responsibility for your own results. Placing blame on someone or something else (e.g. your instructor, your horse, the weather, the footing, etc.) will only keep you stuck in your comfort zone. This does not mean that you should beat yourself up if you don't get the results you expected or wanted. Instead, ask yourself what you need to work on to get a better result. Maybe your horse is not the best match for you right now and you need to practice your skills on a more experienced horse before trying the same exercise or activity with your own horse. Perhaps you need to let your instructor work with your horse for a few sessions to improve his level of training.

Re-framing is another way to expand your comfort zone by changing what you focus on. For example, instead of focusing on your mistakes (no matter how small) or limitations reframe your thinking so that you always find something that went well and focus on that. Success leads to success. Write these positive experiences in your journal. When you are feeling discouraged, you can look back at your achievements to remind yourself how far you have come.

Visualization is a proven technique for achieving your goals and it can be done anytime and anywhere. Visualizing involves not only picturing but also feeling the emotions connected to accomplishing your goals. You are probably already using visualization without realizing it. Whenever you replay that bad experience or picture a bad outcome, you are using visualization. Unfortunately, you are using it to reinforce your fear and negative feelings. Instead, focus on replaying the positive accomplishments you have already achieved and the outcomes you want to achieve.

Complete the following exercise to help create your plan for expanding your comfort zone. Discuss your plan with your Support Team and enlist them to help you stick to it.

Exercise – Create a Plan to Expand Your Comfort Zone

1. Write down some small, baby steps you can add to your routine that will take you out of your comfort zone. Remember that you decide when you are ready to move to each step.

_____

_____

_____

2. Write down a positive riding or horse related experience. Be as detailed as possible including how you felt. Experiencing the emotions is a critical part of the visualization exercise.

_____

_____

_____

3. Identify resources you can use to help support you on your journey. For example, taking riding lessons, going to clinics, getting counseling, etc.

_____

_____

_____

4. List the people who can be on your Support Team. These are people who will encourage you and gently push you without overwhelming you.

_____

_____

_____

"Every time you win, it diminishes the fear a little bit. You never really cancel the fear of losing; you keep challenging it."
~ *Arthur Ashe*

Risk Analysis

There is risk involved with being around and riding horses. Having a healthy fear around them keeps you alert and motivated to keep learning. When you have a healthy fear, there is no reason for you to feel bad because you *'shouldn't be afraid'*. You can pay attention when you start to feel nervous or fearful and rationally determine the level of risk you are taking. Assessing the true risk allows you to determine how valid your fear is.

A risk analysis is simply a personal evaluation of what you feel is risky and the extent of risk you are prepared to accept. For example, one of my clients, Theresa, feels very anxious about riding on trails. She used to enjoy trail riding until her horse bolted while she was on a trail ride with a group of friends. Theresa was so terrified that she jumped off her galloping horse. While she suffered bruising and soreness, she was not seriously injured. Since that experience, Theresa is comfortable only riding in an indoor arena or fenced outdoor ring. For Theresa, riding in a fenced arena is low risk and going trail riding is a very high risk.

Understanding your risk tolerance helps you make rational decisions about where you will ride (in an arena, on the trail, at a show, etc.), when you will ride (i.e. type of footing, the weather conditions, etc) who you will ride with, the type of horse you will ride and what activities you will do with your horse. Factors that will affect these decisions include your health and physical condition, your skill and experience level, your comfort zone, and your horse's training and temperament. For example, if you are planning on going on a trail ride, what is it exactly that you fear might happen? In your risk assessment, you would consider how spooky or quiet your horse is; the weather & footing conditions; the other riders & horses you will be out with; the condition & fit of your tack; your riding skill.

Your risk tolerance can change as you expand your Comfort Zone. Let's take a look at how this would work for my client, Theresa. Riding in an enclosed riding arena is low risk and within her comfort zone. Riding in a fenced field that is larger than the riding arena where she usually rides is a medium risk and moves her out of her Comfort Zone into her Learning Zone. Before riding in the fenced field, Theresa would:

1. Identify the potential hazards associated with riding in this area. Examples - uneven footing; unexpected obstacles; more open space; ground hog or rabbit holes; horse and rider out of comfort zone.

2. Assess the impact of each risk in terms of potential loss and severity. Examples - horse may trip or fall because of uneven footing or hole; horse may bolt in larger space; horse may misbehave because he is in an unfamiliar area; rider may panic and lose control

3. Analyze actions that can be taken to eliminate or reduce the identified risks. Examples – practice walk/halt transitions and steering exercises in the riding ring; explore the field on foot and mark any problem areas and remove debris; use cones to mark a small area of the field that is the 'comfort' zone; watch her trainer ride the horse in the field first; ride her horse with her horse leading or lunging her.

By taking action to gradually expand her comfort zone in the fenced field, Theresa will find that her risk tolerance also expands along with her confidence. Eventually, riding in the fenced field will become a low risk activity and, if she chooses, she can then work towards riding in a more open area or on a trail.

Here are some ideas of ways to reduce the risks involved with horse related activities:

- increasing your knowledge and skill through lessons, clinics and other resources

- learning about horse psychology and behaviour

- working with a competent instructor

- having a trainer work with you and your horse

- wearing appropriate, well fitting riding clothing, boots, gloves and protective equipment (e.g. a properly secured helmet, protective vest)

- ensuring all equipment and tack is in good condition, appropriate for the type of work and fits properly

Complete the exercise on the following page to design your personal risk analysis and plan to minimize risks.

Exercise – Risk Analysis and Plan

Step 1: Write down the activity that you are afraid of but would like
to be able to do and your fear about what might happen. For
each activity, rate the actual level of risk on a scale of 1-10
with 1 being not very likely to happen and 10 being very
likely to happen.

Activity	Potential Risk (What I fear might happen)	Risk Level 1-10

Step 2: For each of your concerns from the first exercise, list the things you can do to eliminate or minimize the risk. Include resources you can use as well as actions you can take.

Potential Risk	Actions & Resources

"A good coach will make his players see what they can be rather than what they are."
~ Ara Parasheghian

Chapter 5 – You Don't Know What You Don't Know

Often when you are struggling with your riding, your relationship with your horse or your confidence, you know something is wrong or missing, but you don't know what it is. You don't know what you don't know. You keep doing things the way you have always done them because you don't know what else to do. But, if you always do what you've always done, you'll always get what you've always got.

We all develop bad habits and sometimes get stuck. There is always something new to be learned. Even Olympic team riders have a coach and they often give and get feedback from their team mates. The best horse people never stop learning and developing their skills.

You need someone to help you and your horse both move forward together. You need a coach. A partner with whom you will have a unique one-on-one relationship. Someone who can help you:

1) Set individual, personal goals and create plans to achieve them.
2) Identify gaps in your knowledge or skills, and figure out the steps needed to fill those gaps.
3) Build upon other training you have had.
4) Enhance your relationship with your horse.
5) Improve your and your horse's performance.

A coach provides you with personalized guidance. He or she supports you by being a resource, a sounding board, and a partner, but also by providing unbiased feedback and by asking questions that spark discussions, provoke thought, and inspire self-reflection.

It is very important to find the right coach for you and your horse. It should be someone who understands where you are now and where you would like to go. He or she should be willing to work with your personal goals.

I recently started coaching a woman (I'll call her Jessie) who was part-boarding a horse with the possibility of buying him. Before starting lessons with me, Jessie was happily going out for rides with another woman on the country roads, through open fields and along wooded trails. She had no fear. That is until one day when her horse spooked at a dog, did a fast 180° turn and galloped back towards home. The saddle slipped and Jessie found herself hanging off the side of her horse unable to get her feet out the stirrups and unable to stop her horse. Fortunately, her horse did stop before Jessie fell off. She was shaken but unharmed. Through this experience, Jessie recognized that she didn't know much about riding and that her lack of knowledge and riding skill could put her as well as her horse in danger.

After Jessie started taking lessons with me, she realized that there was a lot that she didn't know about horses in general as well as about riding:

1. Checking that the tack fit her horse properly (it didn't);
2. Basic riding position (she was off-balance and relying on her stirrups and reins);
3. Reading and feeling the horse's body language (this would have helped her prevent her horse from bolting)

What to Look For in a Coach

Look for a trusted, reputable, professional coach/trainer who is experienced working with adults and dealing with confidence issues. Just because a person is a good rider, horse trainer, has won loads of rewards in competition or has been around horses for most of his or her life does not necessarily make that person a good coach for you. A good coach helps you perform at your best ability by guiding, stimulating and encouraging you to keep growing.

A good coach addresses your issues specifically – even if you are riding in a group. He or she doesn't just focus on what you are doing wrong, but also tells you know when you are doing something right. Your riding lessons should be a positive experience – even if you sometimes struggle.

If you are struggling with a concept or getting your body in a certain position, a good coach will find different ways to explain or show you what he or she means until you get it.

A good coach can clearly explain the 'why' as well as the 'how' so that you can understand the reasons behind what you and your horse are being asked to do.

A good coach is able to work with your horse from the ground and/or in the saddle to demonstrate to you how to do an exercise and what it should look like when you and your horse are doing it correctly. He or she should be able to work through any problems with your horse that you are not ready or able to deal with. A good coach should be able to feel what is happening with your horse so he or she can identify the source of the problem.

A good coach creates a comfortable and positive learning environment for all of his or her students. The focus and attention should always be on you during your lesson. He or she should not be distracted by their cell phone or chatting with other people. You should never be made to feel stupid, intimidated or unimportant. A good coach always treats you and your horse with respect.

A good coach is committed to your success. He or she wants to help you set and achieve your personal goals. He or she will help you avoid frustration by assessing your goals and ensuring they are realistic and that you have a realistic time frame for achieving them.

A good coach's personality and coaching style is compatible with you and your learning style. Know which style of coaching works best for you.

Authoritarian 'Drill Sergeant' Coach – This coach is the 'master' of the lesson. He or she accepts no nonsense, is strict and takes you to boot camp. The lesson is always very structured. The Authoritarian Coach calls all the shots and expects the student to simply follow his or her directions and accept the solutions.

Casual Coach – This coach has a relaxed, easy going style. The lessons may lack structure as this type of coach spends a lot of time listening to the student. He or she may not push you too hard.

Cooperative Coach – This coach encourages the student to have an active role in the lessons and in problem solving. The coach guides the lesson but is flexible in adjusting the strategies and techniques to meet the needs of the student.

Every coach has a predominant style. But, a good coach can adjust when necessary to meet the needs of the student.

A good coach is safety conscious. While helping you develop the techniques and skills to build your confidence and achieve your goals, he or she will always keep you and your horse mentally, emotionally and physically safe. He or she will encourage you to expand your comfort zone without overwhelming you, will push you when needed and will always support you.

Your coach should be able to ride at least one level above you and explain the why as well as the how. It is important that you understand the reasons for the training and not just how it is done. I like to create thinking riders who have a good supply of tools they can apply in different situations. You need to understand what is being asked of you and a good coach will patiently repeat the explanations in different ways if necessary until you get it. It's my job as a coach, to put the information into a form that makes sense to you. That means not just speaking about it, but also demonstrating it and even putting your body in the right way so you can feel it.

A good coach should be able and willing to get on your horse and work through problems. Not being able to do this for my clients was a concern for me when I lost my confidence. It was a strong motivator for me to work through my fear. If I hadn't been able to, I would have given up coaching because I believe that I have no right to ask or expect my students to do something that I cannot do. I often find that getting on a client's horse gives me a better feeling and understanding of what is going on. I can demonstrate the difference between what the client is doing and what I'm asking her to do. This is a very effective teaching method for those people who are visual learners and need to see things to understand them. Sometimes, there may be something subtle that I am not seeing from the ground, but can figure out what is happening once I ride the horse myself. Then I can teach the client how to help her horse.

69

A good coach should be able to honestly assess how realistic your goals are, and help you determine a sensible time frame for achieving them. He or she can help you set S.M.A.R.T. goals (Specific, Measurable, Achievable, Relevant and Timely). Having S.M.A.R.T. goals will help you identify:

5. why your goals are important to you

6. what steps you need to take to achieve your goals

7. what obstacles you may need to overcome

8. possible solutions to any obstacles

9. what resources you will need

Use the goal setting worksheet on the next page to help you set your own S.M.A.R.T. goals.

A good coach will build on the previous lessons as your skills grow adding new challenges as it is appropriate rather than doing the same thing over and over.

Above all, a good coach is committed to helping you be successful, and is willing to take as much time as necessary for that to happen.

SMART Goal Setting Worksheet

Specific | Measurable | Achievable | Relevant | Timely

Draft Goal:

_____

_____

1. **Specific -** What is your desired result? Who, what, where, when, how.

_____

_____

_____

2. **Measurable** – How will you know when you have reached this goal? How can you measure your progress?

_____

_____

_____

3. **Achievable** – What skills are needed? What resources are needed? Does the goal require the right amount of effort?

_____

_____

_____

4. **Relevant** – Is the goal in alignment with your overall desires, mission or strategy?

_____

_____

_____

5. **Timely** – What is the deadline for completing this goal? Is the deadline realistic?

_____

_____

_____

Final Goal:

_____

_____

This goal is important to me because:

_____

_____

_____

_____

The benefits to me of achieving this goal will be:

_____

_____

_____

_____

TAKE ACTION!

Potential Obstacles	**Potential Solutions**
_____	_____
_____	_____
_____	_____
_____	_____
_____	_____

The people who can help me are:

_____

_____

Specific Action Steps: What steps need to be taken to get complete your goal?

Action Step	**Expected Completion Date**	**Completed**
_____	_____	_____
_____	_____	_____
_____	_____	_____
_____	_____	_____
_____	_____	_____

Understand How You Learn

Good coaches understand that people learn best in different ways so they are able to use a variety of modalities to teach different people. There are 3 primary modes of learning. Everyone uses all 3 styles at different times, but we all have one modality that is stronger than the others. The dominant learning modalities are:

- Visual – 25-30%
- Auditory – 25-30%
- Kinesthetic – 15%
- Mixed – 25-30%

If you are a **Visual Learner** you learn best by seeing demonstrations, pictures, videos or reading books. You can picture things clearly in your mind's eye. You probably use expressions like "see what I mean?" and "I see that."

 If you are an **Auditory Learner** you learn best by being told the information. Lecture formats work well for you. You like to discuss things in your own mind. You probably use expressions like "I hear that" or "that sounds right".

If you are primarily a **Kinesthetic/Tactile Learner,** you need to feel (physically and/or emotionally) what you are learning. You learn best if movement is involved. You most likely use phrases like "that feels right" or "I can't get a grip on this".

When you understand how you learn best, you can explain to your coach how you need the information shared with you.

Know Which Stage of Learning You Are In

Learning can be frustrating. Don't be surprised if as you learn how to improve your posture, release tension and pay attention to your horse's movement you suddenly feel like you can no longer ride at all. The reason for this is simple and perfectly natural. There is a process to learning and it takes place in stages. When you understand these 4 stages, you realize that all learning and change do not happen overnight. You will meet some roadblocks along the way. But when you understand that there is process, you will avoid (or at least decrease) frustration as you develop more patience for yourself and your horse.

Four Stages of Learning (Abraham Maslow)

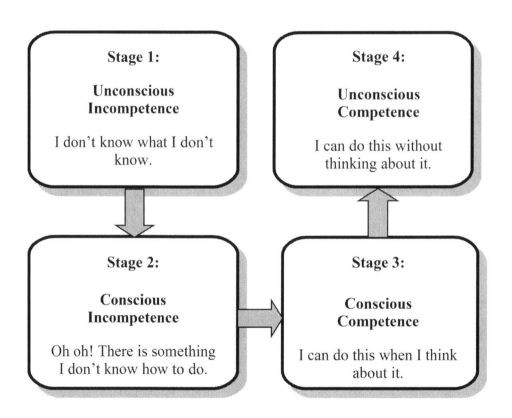

- **Unconscious Incompetence** –At this stage you may recognize that something is not quite right, but you have no idea what it is or how to go about fixing it. You may just have a sense that something is missing. You don't know what you don't know.

- **Conscious Incompetence** – At this stage you are aware that you are having some problems, but you are at a loss as to how to correct them. You might understand what is needed, but are lacking the knowledge or confidence about how to get it. You may even feel overwhelmed by how much you need to learn. You may feel like you are stuck in a rut and are ready to do something about it. You are open to learning new methods, skills or information.

- **Conscious Competence** – At this stage you have taken steps to learn new skills, concepts or practices. It requires effort and mental concentration to do it. It feels unnatural and is outside of your comfort zone. It will take time and practice to become proficient in the new skills.

- **Unconscious Competence** – At this final stage you are comfortable with the new skill that you don't even think about it anymore. It feels natural and has become second nature.

There is no end to learning about horses or riding. It is a journey rather than a destination. When you look at riding this way, you feel frustrated less often as you no longer see obstacles just more opportunities for learning and improving.

Your Horse Needs a Coach

It's difficult for you to work on building your skills and confidence if your horse is green or has behavioural issues that you aren't able to handle or that make you nervous. Your horse's training is just as important to his well-being and development as coaching is to yours. If your horse is young, green or has gaps in his education, he may have behaviours that you are beyond your current skill and knowledge level to address. Having a professional trainer work with your horse will build his confidence and help him become a better partner for you. Ideally, your coach should also be able to work with your horse and you. In some cases, your horse may need more intensive training and you may need to send him to the trainer's facility.

It's crucial to find the right trainer for your horse. In fact, it is one of the most important decisions you will ever make as a horse owner. In North America, horse training is an unregulated industry. That means that anyone can hang out a shingle and call themselves a horse trainer. Many people assume that a high profile, successful, well known trainer or one certified in one of the Natural Horsemanship techniques will not use abusive methods. Unfortunately, it is not very hard to find horror stories of so-called 'professional horse trainers' who have damaged horses physically and psychologically.

What to Look for in a Horse Trainer

A good horse trainer is willing and able to explain the training process to you. He or she may even have a formal contract. If you are sending your horse out to the trainer's facility, you should be welcome to stop by anytime without an appointment to see your horse. Be an active observer by asking questions during or after the training sessions. As your horse improves, do some hands on work with your horse under the trainer's supervision to help increase your knowledge, skill and confidence.

A good trainer wants you to be involved in the training of your horse as much as possible. As a responsible owner, you need to understand not only what your horse has learned from the trainer, but how he was taught. Without the ability to continue with the same methods on your own, you will undo the good training your horse has received. You don't have to be as good as your trainer – if you were, you wouldn't have needed him or her in the first place. You do need to commit to learning and applying the skills and methods to the best of your ability. The better your horse's training is, the more adaptable and tolerant he will be of your mistakes. One of my students looks at it this way - her horse's training is like a bank account. The student makes withdrawals and the trainer makes deposits. When things start to fall apart between you and your horse, it's time to have your coach/trainer make a deposit.

A good trainer knows that it takes as long as it takes to a train a horse – and he or she will tell you that if you ask. Rather than having a 30 or 60 day program that your horse must fit into, the program should be customized for your horse. Just like humans, horses learn at different rates and in different ways.

A good trainer admits that he or she does not know everything there is to know about horses. Nobody knows it all and we are all still learning. At a symposium I attended a couple of years ago, a veterinarian who was making a presentation said, "The more we learn, the more questions we have." A good trainer will have an open mind and continue learning through attending clinics, symposiums, expos and invest in educational materials.

Most importantly, a good trainer makes training a positive experience for your horse. His or her goal is to help your horse learn how to learn and understand what is being asked of him. This can only happen when the trainer works in ways that earn the horse's trust and respect and build the horse's confidence.

You are putting your safety, and that of your horse, in the hands of your coach and/or trainer. So, it is essential that you can relate to him or her and have a relationship of mutual trust and respect. A good coach and trainer works respectfully and patiently with both you and your horse.

There are many resources for finding coaches and trainers:

- ads in equestrian magazines
- postings at feed/tack stores, horse shows
- referrals from friends.
- online bulletin boards and forums

Once you have found potential candidates, contact them by email or phone initially to gather more information about their experience, programs, facility, and fees. Schedule an appointment to visit the coach/trainer, watch him or her teaching a lesson and/or working with a horse. Speak with some of his or her clients.

If you are looking for someone to come to your farm, ask if they will come out to meet you and your horse. Some freelance trainers will give a free consultation or introductory lesson. Don't be afraid to take lessons with different coaches before making your final decision.

Use the check list on the following page as a guide for questions to ask when looking for a riding coach or trainer.

If you're not able to work with a coach on a regular basis, then try to audit or participate in clinic and workshops, attend symposiums, join (or create) a supportive horse owners' group, or get together for educational DVD nights with a group of horse riding friends.

When you keep learning, improving and building your skills in caring for, handling and riding your horse, you build your confidence along the way.

Checklist for Finding a Suitable Coach/Trainer

Stables and Riding Areas	Y	N
Are the stables tidy, clean, well lighted and safe?		
Are the riding areas enclosed?		
Are gates/doors kept closed during lessons/training?		
Are the riding areas free of clutter?		
Do the riding areas have good footing that is not dusty, slippy or too deep?		
Does the indoor riding arena have adequate lighting?		
Equipment		
Are the saddles used on lesson horses fitted with safety stirrups?		
Are students wearing approved riding helmets and proper boots?		
Is the tack used on the horses in good repair?		
Does the tack used on the horses fit properly?		

Horses	Y	N
Do the horses in the coach/trainer's care appear healthy and content?		
Does the coach/trainer handle the horses with care and respect?		
Do horses in training improve by the end of the session?		
Students		
Are students well matched with lesson horses?		
Does the instructor keep focus on the students at all times (eg. No chatting to by-standers or answering cell phone)		
Do students leave the lesson happy?		
Does there appear to be an overall concern about safety and welfare of the horses as well as the riders?		
Does the coach speak to students respectfully and clearly?		
Are you comfortable with the number of people in a group lesson?		

Part 2

UNDERSTAND YOUR HORSE FROM THE GROUND UP

"Love lasts when the relationship comes first."
~ The Buddha

Chapter 6 – Trust Builds Confidence

Confidence is reciprocal between you and your horse. An important factor in determining your level of confidence is your level of trust - in yourself and your abilities, in your horse and in your relationship with each other. You learn to trust each other over time and through shared experiences. You both need to believe that the other will not intentionally hurt you or put you into situations that you can't handle either physically or emotionally. Trust is the glue that holds every relationship together and promotes cooperation. Confidence and healthy relationships will not grow or thrive without a foundation of trust.

A woman came to one of my clinics with her new horse and wanted to establish a better relationship with him. She had lost her previous horse (who she had for many years) through an unfortunate accident. Although her new horse was nice and well trained, he was pushy on the ground and was what I call a 'maybe' horse. A 'maybe' horse is the one that tests a bit to find out if he really has to do as he is being asked. Since this woman had her previous horse for many years, they had established a comfortable and confident relationship because they had many shared experiences and a common language. They understood each other. Her assumption – like so many other new horse owners – was that she would quickly establish the same type of relationship with her new horse. Like most of us, she forgot the time it had taken to establish the relationship she had with her previous horse. She had worked through some challenges with him in the early part of their relationship, but was now only remembering the more recent, happier and cooperative times. Now with her new horse, she had forgotten that trust comes in incremental steps over time. When she recognized this reality, she was able to be more patient with her horse and herself and was willing to go back to working on fundamentals.

Perhaps the most important requirement for building trust is considering the horse's perspective – seeing things from his point of view – so that you can establish a positive relationship. Working with a horse is much like being dropped into a foreign land amongst a tribe of people with different values, a different culture and without a common language. You must first find a way to communicate before you can establish trust and then form a relationship. Having a common form of communication is the bridge that allows connection.

I used to train horses with force, fear and intimidation. I loved them, but I wanted them to work with me on my terms – to do what I wanted, when I wanted and how I wanted. And, I wanted them to learn according to my timeline. There was a lot of focus on my needs and desires. That's no way to build a true partnership. Truth be told, I was using those 'tough' methods to cover up my own fear and feelings of intimidation. After all, horses are very large, powerful animals. They are also unpredictable with a strong flight/fight instinct.

Back in those days, when I was a much less experienced horse woman, I assumed my horse would and should behave the way I wanted because I loved her. After all, I took care of all her physical needs. When she didn't behave as I expected or wanted her to, I would get frustrated sometimes to the point of getting angry with her. I would label her as 'stubborn', 'stupid', or 'lazy'. I would make statements like 'she's just doing it to annoy me' or 'she knows what I want'. My coach would tell me to 'get after her and make her do it', 'you have to show her who the boss is', and 'don't let her know you're afraid'.

When I look back on that time now, I see that I had a pretty one sided mindset about our relationships. I was only looking at it from my own perspective and for what I was getting from it. I did not consider my horse's psychological and emotional needs or what benefit she was getting from our experiences together. I assumed that because I enjoyed it, she did (or should), too. I know now that because of my one sided perspective my horse was not able to trust me.

I know I am not the only person who has behaved this way with her horse. In fact, it is a very common mindset in the horse world. Loads of people expect their horses to behave and perform well simply because they love and care for them. Then they feel disappointed, discouraged and frustrated when that does not happen. Typically, the training techniques used in this type of situation are based on dominance and submission. They can even end up being coercive and forceful. The horse feels bullied and insecure and as a result lacks confidence. This only creates more unpredictable and undesirable behaviour. Taken to the extreme, the horse learns that fighting is useless and just gives in. (This state is called learned helplessness). Horses trained this way may appear to be very obedient, compliant and well trained, but are usually shut down psychologically. They have no emotional connection with humans. When obedience and compliance are gained through fear and intimidation, there is very little, if any, trust and no true respect.

You will not earn your horse's trust and respect by going to the other extreme and being so 'nice' that you have no boundaries. You probably know someone who tries to win her horse's love and affection by always letting the horse have his way. She avoids potential conflict by just not doing things the horse isn't comfortable doing. While the horse may trust that the person will not hurt him, he does not trust that the person will be able to look after his safety and security. He has no respect for this person. This relationship can be compared to that of siblings. One bosses the other around.

Sometimes they get along. Sometimes they fight. People who treat their horses in this manner are often afraid that the horse will not love them if they set boundaries. But the reality is that your horse needs boundaries and a clear social hierarchy to feel safe, secure and confident.

The problem that both of these examples illustrate is that a positive, trusting and confident relationship cannot be established with your horse when you look at the relationship only from the perspective of your needs and desires without considering those of the horse.

A whole new level of relationship with horses opened up to me when I learned from Chris Irwin how to work with the rules, psychology and body language that make sense to the horse. These techniques honour the horses' way of being in the world. I learned to work with their nature instead of against it. I developed a holistic approach of working with the horse and the human so that they both benefit from the experiences together.

By changing my perspective, I was able to create a deep, true and willing partnership with horses that was focused on mutual trust and respect. It was life changing. I learned that nothing changes until you change. And, I regretted that it had taken me so long to see that it is not possible for the horse to understand the human perspective. It is possible for us to learn to understand his.

My greatest teacher of this lesson has been my gelding, Ever Sacred. A Medicine Hat Paint with a 'bring it on' attitude. I have known him since he was a foal and he was born with this challenging temperament. And by that I mean he challenges everything. His first answer to every request was 'no'. Ask him to walk forward and he would plant all four feet and refuse to move. Increase the pressure and he would fling his head up and back as if he was trying to knock me off his back. If I had still been using my previous mindset and methods when working with Ever, our training sessions would have escalated into fear, stress and aggression on both sides.

I would have yelled, kicked, spurred, and whipped him. And felt justified to do so. Instead I would focus on getting him to move just one foot in any direction. It didn't matter how far we moved only that we moved. It also mattered **how** we moved. Yes, I had to have firm, clear and consistent boundaries, but I also had to find ways to work with him that built his trust and respect for me while helping him to be calm, focused and lose his resistance. It took time and patience. It was frustrating at times, but also very rewarding. Ever would test me every time I worked with him. Each time I had to pass his test and then we would move forward. Over time, his tests got shorter and easier. Eventually, he didn't need them anymore. We understand each other. We trust each other. We respect each other. We are true partners.

With a deeper understanding of horse behaviour, herd dynamics and equine body language, you not only understand why your horse does what he does, but you are able to proactively prevent unwanted behaviour rather than reactively waiting for the "bad thing" to happen. You will be calmer and more focused – and so will your horse. Your behaviour will be more consistent and predictable. You will have a common language that will be the bridge to establishing a positive relationship. All of these pieces put together help your both to build your confidence – in yourselves and in each.

By working with your horse or any horse in this way, you earn the horse's trust. You earn his respect. You build his confidence as well as your own. His behaviour becomes more predictable. Your behaviour becomes more predictable to him. Your horse becomes a willing, relaxed and confident partner.

Establishing and maintaining a healthy relationship with your horse requires you to honour and respect your horse as a horse. Whether you are interacting with him from the ground or in the saddle, you earn your horse's trust and respect by:

1. Establishing a common language

2. Having clear and consistent boundaries

3. Letting him know you will never intentionally hurt him

4. Letting him know you will always keep him safe.

The Foundation of Trust

Your horse is always aware of your movements, your emotions and your energy and will be affected – for better or for worse – by them. He is a genius at reading you at the most subtle level. You can't fool him. If you try to cover up your fear with anger, he will sense the incongruence and be mistrustful. It is far better for both of you to admit you are feeling nervous or flat out terrified (or somewhere in between). Horses – like most people – appreciate honesty and authenticity.

Your thoughts and emotions affect how you move as well as your level of awareness. When you are nervous, upset or angry your movements are stealthy, hurried or erratic. These types of movements unsettle your horse because they mimic predatory movements. Predators move with stealth when they are sneaking up on prey. Hurried and erratic movements could signal a predator leaping to attack their prey.

Think about your bad day at the office, the fight you had with your spouse, or all the chores you need to get done by the end of the day and notice how you feel. While you're focused on the thoughts inside your head, you cannot be fully aware of your surroundings or your horse. This is also true if you are distracted by conversations you are having with your friends in the barn or while you are riding. If your horse turns off his awareness, he is shut down. He might look like he is completely oblivious to what's going on around him

and that he's dozing on the cross-ties while you groom him. Then suddenly 'without warning' he flies back breaking his halter. You are standing there wondering why he blew up over nothing. If he is not shut down, he reacts to your movements because he is trying to read what you're saying to him - even if you don't think you are saying anything to him. It is like he is autistic and he is over stimulated and reactive to all the 'noise' and 'static' he is picking up from you – physically and energetically.

To build trust with your horse, you must develop a deeper understanding of equine body language so that you can better read him and know how he reads you. You need to be able to use your body in a way that makes sense to him. This means you must develop and maintain awareness of your own physical and emotional states as well as those of your horse at all times.

Remember that nothing changes until you change.

1. Awareness

You develop your awareness through practice, practice and more practice. Spend some time just watching your horse interact with his herd mates. Let go of your preconceived notions and just observe. Look for the subtle signs they use to communicate with each other – a flick of an ear, pinched nostrils, the swish of a tail. All movements have some meaning.

In the wild, each individual horse's survival depends upon their level of awareness for their environment and their herd mates. As prey animals, they have to be aware of predators before they get too close. As herd animals, they have to be aware of the communication within the herd. The horse that is last to notice the signals that the wolves are hunting or the warning signal from his herd mates might just be the first one going for dinner with the wolves.

a) Practice being aware of what is going on within the environment at all times. Only then can your horse believe that you are alert and aware enough to notice and protect him from potential danger.

b) Your horse is aware of every move you make and reads even your must subtle body language. In fact, he is a genius at reading body language. So, it is important that you are aware of your own body movements at all times and how your horse is interpreting those movements. If you send conflicting, mixed or inconsistent messages through your body movements, your horse will be confused and unable to trust you.

c) In the same way, you must always be aware of your horse's body language – even the subtleties of twitches and muscle tension - to interpret how he is feeling.

2. Boundaries

Watch a group of horses interacting in the paddock and you will notice that they do not pull each other around. They push and block each other with their bodies – body to body. This behaviour is an important part of their herd dynamics. They do not tell each where to go but rather where not to go. The horse that pushes another horse into a boundary is the better horse because the horse that has been pushed into a boundary cannot run away. Being between "a rock and a hard place" is not a good place to be for a prey animal.

There are 3 types of boundaries that are necessary for establishing mutual trust, respect and confidence with our horses.

a) The most important boundary to establish with your horse is your personal space. The alpha horse does not get bitten or kicked, pushed or blocked by any other horse in the herd. She can go anywhere she likes, take the best food, move other horses away from the water supply and not be challenged. If your horse rubs on you with her head, nips you, threatens to kick or strike you, pushes you with her shoulder or barrel, leans into you or pins her ears when you go into her stall, she is seeing you the same way she sees a lower ranking herd mate. Ask your horse to respect your personal space by setting boundaries that clearly, firmly and consistently tell her to not come into your 'bubble'. You decide how big it is. With an excited, aggressive or pushy horse, your bubble of personal space should be quite large – at least a horse length. With a passive, gentle, calm horse, your personal space can be very small – an arm's length or less.

b) It is important for you to respect your horse's personal space - the bubble around her head and neck. This area is the particularly vulnerable area that the horse naturally wants to protect. I equate that area on the horse to the intimate areas of our own bodies.

Just as the horse has to earn enough trust to be allowed into your personal space, you must earn enough trust from your horse to be allowed into her personal space. Next time you go to stroke your horse's face, notice her reaction. Is she enjoying it, tolerating it or anxious about it? If she gently leans into your touch and half closes her eyes, those are signs that she is enjoying the interaction. However, if she stands slightly braced, raises her head even a bit, those are signs she is only tolerating the interaction. If she moves her head away from your touch, steps away from you or pushes your hand away, those are signs she is anxious about the interaction. There are times when you need to work around and handle your horse's head. But how you approach that area makes a big difference to your horse and how she feels about you. Be aware of your posture and the energy you are sending when you are near her head and neck. Avoid sending impulsive (pushing) energy into that area. Keep your body soft and imagine the energy being pulled away from your horse. (I talk more about how horses read energy in Chapter 7 "Posture and Body Language".)

c) Whenever you work with your horse using a halter or bridle, leading, lunging or riding, contact through the rope or reins creates boundaries that tell your horse where not to go. Contact creates a consistent connection between you and your horse. Contact never pulls but instead uses resistance to block movements that you don't want. For example, the right rein does not pull your horse's head to the right. The right rein blocks your horse from turning her head to the left. The left rein does not pull your horse's head to the left. It blocks your horse from turning her head to the right.

3. Consistency

Your horse is reading you as soon as she can see you not just when you are working with her. She doesn't know if you don't know her language and social rules. If you don't make sense to her, she won't be able to trust you. Instead, she will tune you out, push you around or be terribly insecure and flighty around you.

Just like us, horses become insecure and anxious when they do not know what to expect. You can help your horse feel secure and safe with you when your behaviour and the rules you set are consistent in all situations. Whether you are on the ground or in the saddle, apply the same rules every time and every moment you are with your horse.

Your horse gets confused when you sometimes allow a particular behaviour and other times you do not allow it. For example, when you are calm, in a good mood or wearing your old sweat shirt you allow her to rub her head on you after you have removed her bridle. However, you get upset with her if she does the same thing when you are in a rush, stressed or wearing your show jacket. In the same way, she gets confused when your aids or cues are not clear or you sometimes mean it and sometimes do not. For example, let's say you are riding your horse and want her to turn left. But she resists your aids and pulls the reins to go right. If you eventually allow her to turn right, she learns that by resisting hard enough or long enough you will give in and allow her to have her way. This inconsistency teaches her to not respect your direction and creates more resistance in her.

Remember that your relationship with your horse starts from the ground and from the moment your horse can see you. Horses don't miss a thing. In the wild, their survival depends on their level of awareness of their herd mates, their ability to communicate through body language and their awareness of their environment. If you want to develop a better relationship with your horse, start applying these 3 simple steps - Awareness, Boundaries and Consistency - and you will be well on your way to creating a mutually trusting and respectful relationship with your horse.

Horse Psychology

The herd and prey psychology of horses affects everything about their behaviour. As prey animals, they are concerned for their safety every single moment and their strong flight or fight instinct causes many of the behaviours we do not understand. That is why it is so important to address the root cause of your horse's behaviour rather than simply dealing with the symptomatic behaviour.

According to horseman, Chris Irwin, there are 4 psychological rules of the equine mind:

1) Authority (respect & trust) must not be assumed, but must be earned through the integrity of your actions
2) Where we go doesn't matter. What matters most is how we go there.

3) When conflict happens pushing my body is ok. Getting in my face is not.
4) Never tell me where to go. Give me boundaries about where not to go.

By understanding and applying these rules to your relationship with your horse, you can develop mutual trust and respect – the foundation of a healthy partnership – and become the better horse in your horse's mind.

Herd Dynamics

Horses need the security of the herd for their survival. In the wild, solitary horses are vulnerable to predators. Herds have a specific structure and each horse knows where his/her place is within that group. Knowing where a horse fits into the herd and interacts with other herd members will give you clues to how the horse will be with you.

Even in a herd of 2 (you & your horse), the horse needs to know who is the leader. If it isn't you, it is your horse. By learning how to be a benevolent leader you can build a trusting and respectful relationship with your horse that builds confidence in both of you. Leadership built on fear based dominance will never result in this same level of confidence.

Being able to become the better horse – the respected, trusted and benevolent leader that your horse needs and desires - requires that you develop:

- the ability to stay mentally present (be in the moment);

- awareness for interpreting your horse's feelings through his or her body language;

- self-awareness for what you are feeling and communicating through your own body language; and,

- ongoing awareness for what is happening in the environment.

Equine Body Language

As herd animals, horses rely on body language as their main form of communication. They use it to determine herd dynamics as well as to warn of potential danger. Their ability to send and receive messages across distance without making any sound is important for keeping them safe from predators. As a result, horses are very finely tuned in to even the most subtle body movements and changes of energy. An alpha mare can send a message with a quick flick of her tail, a movement of her ears or a change in her posture.

Most people with even minimal experience with horses recognize the basic signals given by the horse's ears. Pinned back ears mean anger. Ears pricked forward show interest. Floppy ears signify calmness. However, as you develop more awareness of the more subtle cues as well as the combinations of signals given from multiple body parts (i.e the ears, eyes, mouth, nostrils, tail and posture), you will be able to more precisely read how your horse is feeling in any given moment. Not only that, but you will also be able to change how your horse is feeling by working with him to change his posture.

Horses' physical and mental states are completely connected (horses don't lie about how they are feeling). A horse who is stressed mentally will show it in his body posture and movement. A horse who becomes stressed through his body by being "bent out of shape" will quickly become mentally stressed as well. When you know which postures are stressful and which ones feel good, you can change how your horse feels mentally by changing his physical shape. You can also learn how to use your body to communicate with your horse in a way that makes sense to him.

Horses communicate through their bodies and truly live in their bodies. Their physical shape mirrors their mental shape. They don't pretend to be one thing when they are feeling another – that is a particularly human trait. We can feel sad, but put on a "happy face". Horses cannot. They simply do not have any concept of this incongruence between emotions and physicality.

As well as body shape, equine body language uses 3 types of energy which are directed at 5 specific areas of the body.

The 3 energies are:

1) Pushing (impulsive, forward);

2) Blocking (stopping movement); and.

3) Drawing (open, receiving).

Pushing and Drawing tell the horse where to go while Blocking tells them where not to go.

The 5 areas of the body are:

1) corner of the mouth,

2) shoulder,

3) barrel,

4) flank

5) hip

You may have noticed that in most conflicts between horses bite and kick marks appear on the body from the shoulders to the hips. They rarely appear on the head and neck. This "no go zone" is the most vulnerable area of the body that horses want to protect and, generally, respect among each other. (Note: If you have a horse with bites on his neck, you probably have an overly aggressive bully in the herd.) We can relate the "no go zone" to our own bubble of personal space. The less familiar we are with someone, the larger that bubble becomes.

Pushing energy is used to move other horses and is directed to a specific area of the body, (but not to the head or neck) for a specific purpose. Pushes can come from the head, shoulder, barrel or hips and be sent to the shoulder (move your front end away), barrel (bend away from me), flank (go forward) or hips (move your hind end away). A respectful horse will comply by moving as directed. A disrespectful or challenging horse will push back at the push.

The two photographs (below and on the next page) show three geldings communicating through their body shapes and energy.

In the photo below, the horse on the left of the photo is pushing the other 2 horses forward as he charges straight up from behind them. The Paint's barrel is bent into the horse on the right as he sends a push from his shoulder in to the "no go zone". That horse responds with ears pinned back while rearing and at the same time bending his body away from the Paint. Although he is displaying displeasure, the big horse has yielded to the Paint's push.

In the photo below, the horse on the left has his hips angled towards (pushing) the other 2 horses. The Paint has yielded his hips to this push. While drawing his hips away from the horse on the left, he is pushing them into the horse on the right. The Bay (right of photo) has yielded his shoulders to the Paint's pushing hind quarters.

Horses read us the same way they read other horses. However, they read us vertically (head to toe) and other horses horizontally (head to tail). But, they still read the energy coming from our bodies (head, shoulders, arms, hips, and core). To get a better understanding of how this works try the following simple 2 part exercise with your horse.

Pushing & Drawing Energy Exercise

Part 1:

Have your horse on a loose lead rope. Stand on his left side between his shoulder and nose. Put your weight into your right leg so that your right hip is pushing towards him. In a short time and, depending on your horse's temperament and relationship with you, he will respond by either raising his head, turning his nose away from you, bringing his nose towards you to push or maybe even nip at you, or backing up. As he bends away from you, his shoulder will be pushing into your space. If you move out of the way to avoid being stepped on, your horse will see you as ranking lower than him because you yielded your space to his pushing energy.

In this exercise, you are standing in your horse's "no go zone". You are rudely sending pushing (impulsive) energy from your hip into her neck. This is typical of what happens between people and horses when we are unaware of the rules of equine body language. Our alignment and body shape cause the horse to take the head away and push the body into us. We then fix what we have caused by pulling the head back towards us. If we follow the sequence of possible events, the horse is now set up to step into the person's space. In this scenario, the person either steps out of the horse's way (subordinate response), hits the horse for "being rude" (reactive sore loser) or yanks on the lead rope to make the horse stand still (aggressive bully).

The incongruence between our body language and our behaviour is confusing to the horse. Our horses cannot trust us when we are inconsistent and will not respect us when we show subordinate or bullying behaviour. The horse feels insecure and unsafe which results in nervousness, resistance and/or conflict.

Pushing & Drawing Energy Exercise

Part 2:

Get into the same alignment as in Part 1, but shift your weight to your left leg and open your right hip so that it is drawing away from your horse. Wait a short time for your horse to respond. She will bring her nose to centre or gently towards you and lower her head. In this shape, you are showing respect for your horse's personal space by creating drawing (receiving) energy from your open hip. The horse feels physically and mentally calm, respectful, and balanced. The square front feet show that she is physically and mentally in park (not thinking about moving). The horse and the person are mutually bent away from each other – neither pushing into the others space. This is the shape you will see two friendly horses take when they are beside each other.

Your horse's temperament will affect the timing of his response as well as how he responds. A truly forgiving horse will take longer to react to our rude body shape in part 1 of this exercise. A stoic horse could take longer to respond to the polite draw in Part 2 – particularly right after you have been in his no go zone.

To earn your horse's trust and respect – and the role as benevolent leader – requires that you become the better horse. Because the best horse is the most aware horse, you need to develop a keen awareness of yourself (mentally as well as physically), your horse (reading body language), and your environment (what is going on around you). As you become more consistent in this silent communication with your horse, you will be on your way to having the relationship of partnership and friendship that you have been looking for.

Standing in your horse's "no go zone" sends pushing energy from your body into his head and neck. A passive horse will take his head away from you. With his head up, he is in "alert" mode and feels stressed.

Opening your hip nearest to your horse's head creates drawing energy that invites the horse to bring his nose towards you and lower his head. In this shape, your horse feels calm and more comfortable being with you.

"We have almost forgotten how strange a thing it is that so huge and powerful and intelligent an animal as a horse should allow another, and far more feeble, animal to ride upon its back."

~ Peter Gray

Chapter 7 - Boundaries – "With All Due Respect"

Establishing clear personal boundaries helps to keep both you and your horse safe. A good boundary simply defines 'your space' and 'my space'.

In all relationships, clearly defined and consistent boundaries create structure, maintain order, enhance safety and define acceptable and unacceptable behaviour. Individuals with clear boundaries present a sense of confidence, self assurance and self respect. If boundaries are non-existent, inconsistent or not respected, the result is a sense of insecurity, discomfort, tension, mistrust and disrespect.

The need for respect of personal boundaries is reciprocal – whether person to person, horse to horse or person to horse. You need your horse to respect your boundaries, and he needs you to respect his.

In healthy relationships, we unconsciously know and abide by the rules of personal space. As the diagram on the next page illustrates, the comfortable distance between you and a person changes depending on how well you know each other. We all know that feeling of discomfort when someone inappropriately encroaches on our personal space. It's the same for our horses.

When we interact with other humans our smallest 'bubble' extends out and all around our bodies about 18 inches. We are comfortable only with close family and friends and our own pets in this 'Intimate Space'. We get uncomfortable if an acquaintance or even worse a stranger comes into this space. The next bubble extends from 18 inches to 4 feet outwards. Friends and acquaintances can comfortably hang out in this 'Personal Space'. A stranger standing this close gives us the willies. From 4 to 12 feet out is our 'Social Space' where we are comfortable carrying out routine social interactions with new acquaintances or complete strangers.

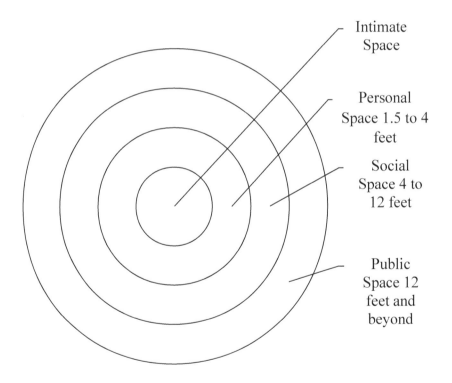

Intimate Space

Personal Space 1.5 to 4 feet

Social Space 4 to 12 feet

Public Space 12 feet and beyond

Beyond that bubble is 'public space' which is open to everyone.

Our horses have the same types of 'bubbles' around them. We need to respect the social rules about personal space with our horses just as we do with people. We also need to ask our horses to respect our personal space.

If your horse is exhibiting any of the following behaviours, it's time to check your boundaries:

- pushiness, biting, flightiness and/or spooking;
- being defiant, sullen or shut down;
- ignoring or challenging you.

Horses have social structure that shares many similarities with human social structure. Part of understanding and working with the horses' social rules means paying setting and respecting the boundaries that are an essential part of equine communication and herd dynamics.

The first boundary you must understand and respect is the "no go zone" around the head and neck. This bubble comes out of one shoulder at a 45 degree angle, goes about 1 inch away from the nose and then back to the other shoulder at a 45 degree angle. It is similar to our 'intimate space'. Assuming to touch or pat a horse on his head or neck is the same as an acquaintance or stranger giving you a hug.

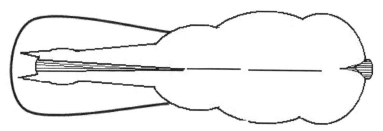

The bubble around your horse's neck and head
is his 'Intimate Space'.

Another important zone to be aware of with horses is the "girth line". This "line of respect" is located on the barrel approximately where the saddle girth/cinch goes.

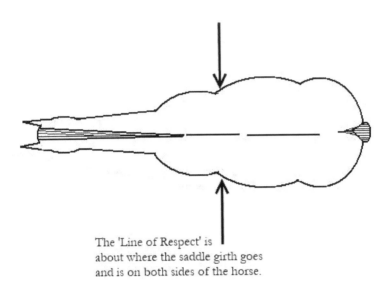

The 'Line of Respect' is about where the saddle girth goes and is on both sides of the horse.

Watch horses interacting with each other in a field or paddock. A respectful horse will not take his girth line past a higher ranking horse's girth line. If he does "cross the line", he will do so passively with a lowered head and his barrel bent away from the other horse. One horse challenging another will pass more aggressively with a high head and his body bending into the other horse. In the latter case, the higher ranking horse will reprimand the offender. Horses read this girth line on humans as the midline running from our ear through our shoulder, hip and heel (where the outside seam of your jeans is located).

Another component of equine social structure is creating movement and yielding space. Horses push each other around to determine their place in the herd hierarchy. The horse who moves out of another horse's way (yields his space) is lower in the hierarchy. The horse that gets pushed into a physical boundary (e.g. fences, walls, trees, etc.) is in a more vulnerable position because he is trapped. The horse who did the pushing ranks higher in the herd. These same rules apply in your little herd of two – you and your horse.

Horses are always aware of these body language & herd rules and it is the only way they know how to perceive and make sense of the world. So, if your horse's movement causes you to move out of his way or pushes you into a physical boundary, he perceives you as below him in the herd order and not worthy of his respect. The same rules apply whether you on are on the ground or riding. Since our relationships with our horses start from the ground up, it is best to first establish boundaries from there.

Ground Work Exercise – Earning Respect

1. Define Your Personal Space – Whether you are leading your horse, entering his stall or grooming him in the cross-ties, create an imaginary bubble around yourself to define your personal space. Do not allow your horse to move into your space with any part of his body unless you have invited him there. His body should never bend into you, but should be straight or bent around you.

   If your horse is pushy, disrespectful, mentally unfocused or aggressive, make the space as large as necessary to keep you safe from potential bites or strikes. If necessary, use a dressage or lunge whip to lengthen your reach. Think of it as your arm extender.

2. Respect Your Horse's Personal Space – Be aware and respectful of your horse's "no go zone" and do not send any impulsive, forward energy directly towards his head or neck.

If you are standing in front of your horse when he moves into your space, your push should be directed at his chest to tell him to back away from you.

If you are standing beside him, the push should be directed towards his shoulder or hip whichever is moving towards you. Keep your own safety in mind and use your "arm extender" (the whip) so that you are not within striking or kicking distance. Just match the level of energy your horse is using. Too much energy may provoke fear or aggression. Too little energy will not be respected.

3. Stand Your Ground - If your horse is pushy, stand your ground and put up a block with your hand or whip towards his body (not to his head). Ask him to back out of your space by waving the whip horizontally towards his body, tap him with the lash end or use the handle for a firm, end for a firm, direct push.

While you should always enforce your boundaries whenever you are with your horse, a good time to practice and become more comfortable with doing so is when your horse is cross-tied.

Many horses become agitated and anxious when tied. Their mental stress is exhibited through their physical shape. Horses who are busy when tied have an unbalanced frame – scissored legs, high head, dropped or hollow back. This frame keeps them in flight mode. With adrenaline pumping into the blood stream, his level of stress and anxiety level as well as his need to move will be increased.

Exercise – Create Calmness in the Cross Ties:

If your horse is very stressed about being tied, start with him just on a lead rope so that you can allow him to move when necessary to help release the stress he is feeling. If you are using cross-ties, ensure they are long enough to allow your horse to bring is neck to level (poll same height as withers) without becoming tight. You will apply boundaries to encourage – not force – your horse to stand quietly, straight, square and level.

How long this takes depends upon your horse's level of anxiety and respect for your boundaries. The aim is to bring him into a straight, square, level headed frame which will create a feeling of calm in him physically and mentally. Although this exercise is simple, it may not be easy at first.

1) Focus on Straight, Square & Level:

a. <u>Straight</u>

Your horse is straight when his spine is in alignment from nose to tail. He will find and feel this straightness when his left hind foot lines up directly behind the left fore foot and the right hind lines up directly behind the right fore.

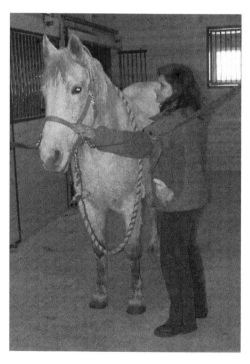

Ask your horse to stand straight by pushing the appropriate hip or shoulder into alignment. If his barrel bends into you, gently press on his girth (about where your heel sits when riding). As soon as your horse moves away from your push stop pushing.

b. Square

When the front feet are square, your horse is more balanced. Getting all 4 feet square is the ideal, but getting the front feet square is adequate. As you correct your horse's straightness, he may stand square on his own. When he stands scissored ask him to step one foot backwards or forwards. For backwards, push on the front

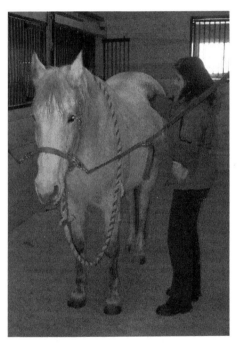

of the shoulder of the leg you want him to move. For forwards, gently tap his flank. Keep repeating one foot at a time until he finds square.

c. Level headed

Encourage your horse to bring his neck to level by gently rocking his head laterally (side to side) with slight downward pressure. Avoid using force by pulling or pushing his head as this will create more stress and resistance. Use a rhythmic swinging movement with the intent of relaxing his neck. Place your hands on the cross ties, directly on the sides of his halter, the bridge of his nose, or use a lead rope attached to the bottom ring of his halter. If you horse tries to raise his head or turn it left or right, use your hand or hands in the same places to block his movement.

Encourage your horse to lower his neck by gently rocking his head laterally (side to side) with slight downward pressure.

2) Be Aware of Your Body Language, Alignment & Energy

Since horses are very tuned in to physical and emotional energy it is important to be aware of your own body shape and mental state. Set the boundaries clearly, calmly and consistently without becoming aggressive, angry or submissive. Make sure that pushing energy from your body (arms, hips, core) is only directed at his body and never towards his head or neck.

3) Stay in the moment

Let go of time frames and expectations and put your focus only on what is happening moment to moment. Your horse may stand quietly for a few seconds only to be distracted by something and changing his shape. Just ask him to come back to straight, then square, then level.

By enforcing clear and consistent boundaries, you will enhance your relationship with your horse, bring him into a relaxed physical shape which will be reflected in a calm mental state, and put you both in a better frame of mind. As you do this for him consistently over and over, he will begin to associate feeling calm and safe with being with you.

Remember that you are training your horse even if you are not consciously thinking about it. Every minute you are with your horse – even if you are separated by the paddock fence or stall wall - is training time. If he can see you, he is reading you. Be aware of the messages you are sending him.

Good training takes time and requires consistency on your part. You cannot achieve behavioural change nor build trust and respect by rushing or being impatient. Your horse will respect your boundaries if you respect your own need for them and show respect for his.

"At its finest, rider and horse are joined not by tack, but by trust. Each is totally reliant upon the other. Each is the selfless guardian of the other's very well-being."

~ *Unknown*

Chapter 8 – Equine Mind and Body Language

Your horse's frame of body and behaviour tell you exactly how he is feeling mentally. His frame of body equals his frame of mind. His behaviour is his communication. From his nose to his tail, his posture, energy and focus are messages about how he is feeling physically and mentally. There is a reason and a meaning for everything he does So, if your horse is dancing in the cross ties, trying to bite you or stepping into your space, he is not simply being "rude". These behaviours are symptoms of his anxiety, fear or resistance to what is happening. If your horse stands quietly, but stoically without blinking or responding to you, he is shut down and is tuned out. If your horse stands calmly and relaxed, aware of what is going on around him and also paying attention to you, you have quality bonding time happening. Not only can you can read all of this information to recognize how your horse is feeling at any moment, you can also change his frame of mind by changing his physical frame.

Posture (how you hold your body) is an important part of body language in both humans and horses. It conveys a wealth of information about how an individual is feeling emotionally and also provides hints about personality characteristics such as confidence, openness, submissiveness, aggressiveness, etc.

Imagine two people attending a business meeting. One person is interested in what is going on. The other is bored or indifferent. You know which is which just through the body posture. The person who is interested will be sitting up straight. The one who is bored will have her body hunched forward or be slouching in her chair.

Our ability to interpret posture in other humans is an integral part of our social interactions and happens mostly at an unconscious level. Posture where the upper body is open and exposed indicates confidence, friendliness, openness and willingness. Closed posture makes the person smaller as if they want to hide by hunching forward and crossing the arms and legs. It indicates hostility, unfriendliness, anxiety or lack of confidence.

Your posture signals to the world your emotional state. That's why you know whether it's a good time to ask your boss for time off or if you should wait. You can see when your spouse, child or friend needs a hug because they are feeling down and vice versa. People will feel comfortable or uncomfortable approaching you based on your posture. Horses respond in the same way.

But, there is more power in posture than just reading what you see. For both you and your horse, changing your posture changes how you feel. There is a reciprocal connection between mind and body. Changing your state of mind affects your posture and how you feel physically, but changing your physical state also changes your state of mind and how you feel mentally. It's an ongoing cycle.

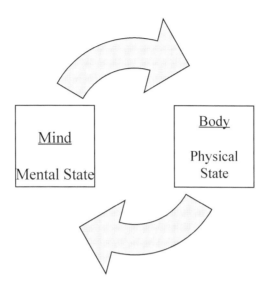

Try this simple exercise to feel for yourself how your posture affects how you feel mentally and physically. Sit or stand with a closed posture. Fold your torso slightly forwards, hunch your shoulders, and breathe with shallow breaths. Notice how you feel after holding this posture for only a couple of minutes. Now shake off that posture. Sit or stand up straight, with your chin and chest lifted, your shoulders open and take deep, slow breaths. Notice how you feel now. Which feels better, more powerful? The open posture is the posture of confidence.

Any posture whether good or bad can become a habit. Many years ago, I had an office job that required many hours of sitting at a desk working on a computer every day. As is typical for many office workers, I didn't pay attention to my posture and would sit with a rounded back, hunched shoulders and my chin to chest. At the end of the day, I would be more stiff and sore than if I had been working with the horses. As this posture became a habit, it affected how I sat on a horse, as well. I had to develop awareness for my posture and correct it regardless of what I was doing – sitting at my desk, driving, walking. I created the habit of maintaining correct posture. You can practice good posture whether sitting or standing by engaging your core to support your torso, keeping your shoulders open, your shoulders aligned over your hips and your chin parallel to the ground.

Because horses also have the same a mind/body connection, it is possible for you to help change how your horse feels emotionally by changing his physical shape. Frame of body truly is frame of mind – there is no separation of either. Whether your horse is mentally stressed – anxious, afraid or angry- or feeling calm and relaxed, his posture will tell you. Unlike humans, horses don't fake their emotions or how they feel. Being able to read all the signals from your horse's nose to his tail will give you a clear picture of how he honestly feels.

Frame of Body Affects Frame of Mind

In horses, posture is often referred to as 'frame' and applies to the shape that is created by the topline – the spine and muscles along the withers, back and loins – along with the position of the head and neck.

Horses can also develop bad habits in their postures through poor training and riding or ongoing interactions with other horses. Poor postures cause tension, stress and strain to the muscles and joints. Healthy, natural postures enhance the horse's natural movement, and improve strength and suppleness. These 'feel good' postures are the ones you must encourage your horse to carry himself in.

Following is a list of the 5 different frames that horses may take. The first 4 are postures that are natural to horses. The last one is only created with human intervention.

1. Long & Low - poll lower than withers

2. Level - poll level with withers

3. High Headed with Lifted Back – poll above withers; back and neck round

4. High Headed with Hollow Back – poll above withers; back dropped or concave

5. Round Poll with Hollow Back - nose pulled into chest; back dropped or concave

The first 3 frames (Long and Low, Level, and High Headed with Lifted Back) are the most beneficial for the horse and for working with your horse. The fourth frame, while a natural shape, is a posture that creates stress in the lumbar thoracic area (where the saddle sits) and also creates the flow of adrenaline. Horses use this posture naturally to intimidate other horses. If they spend a lot of time in this frame they will make themselves sore.   Any frame in which the horse's back is hollow creates mental as well as physical tension. It also stresses and strains his joints and muscles. It affects his ability to perform well and over time can cause unsoundness, lameness and chronic pain.

The last frame (Round Poll with Hollow Back) is the only shape that is completely created through human intervention. The horse's nose comes behind the vertical and in extreme cases may touch the chest. It is created by using training techniques that focus on the front end or the "head set" of the horse. Pressure applied from the reins or gadgets such as martingales, side reins or draw reins to bring the head and neck into the desired position creates what some people see as a beautiful neck position; however they also create an incorrect and unhealthy posture with a hollow back, disengaged hindquarters and stressed, tense dorsal muscle chain (neck extensors, longissimus dorsi, gluteal and hamstring muscles). This frame is harmful to the horse's well-being as it causes both physical and mental stress, resistance and imbalance in the horse. Over time, the physical stress results in deterioration of muscles and stress to joints which can cause chronic pain and lameness.

Long & Low is the posture of a passive, calm and relaxed horse. It's the natural posture of dozing or grazing. It signals to another horse that "I'm not a threat". As the neck lowers (poll lower than withers), the back naturally lifts to level, the muscles in the neck and back are gently stretched and the vertebrae open allowing unrestricted passage of the spinal cord and nerves creating a feeling of calm - physically and mentally. If the horse is moving in this posture, he is balanced and supple, his hindquarters are engaged as they reach well under his body, and his weight is lifted off his forehand. When a horse is in this posture, he is much less reactive to external stimuli. So, a horse being lead, lunged or ridden in this frame will be more relaxed and less likely to react with behaviours like spooking, bucking or bolting.

Level is the next posture of a calm horse, but when he has more focus than the dozing or grazing horse. When the horse's poll is level with his withers, his back is also level but not stretching in the same was as it does when he is long and low. This more neutral position lets the horse develop more impulsion, balance and athleticism. As with the long and low frame, the horse is less likely to have big reactions to external distractions.

The photos on the next page show the same horse walking in the natural frames of 'long and low' and 'level'.

Below: The natural frame of long and low at the walk. Note how far the right hind leg reaches under the horse's body. The weight is off his forehand, his back is lifted, and his poll is below his withers.

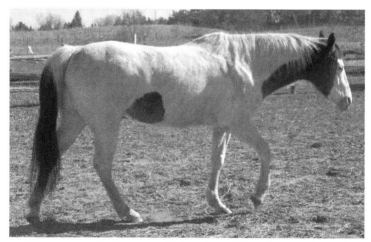

Above: The natural frame of level. The horse has the same engagement as the previous photo while his poll is now level with his withers.

High headed and lifted back is the posture of a more focused horse. It is important to note that while his head and neck are elevated, his back is still lifted. In this frame, the horse's hind legs are still able to reach well underneath him. His nose is at or slightly in front of the vertical.

Above: The natural frame of high head and level back at the trot. The left hind leg reaches well under his body (tracking up to his front foot print), his weight is lifted off the forehand, his back is level and his poll is higher than his withers. The horse's ears are pricked forward focused on something in front of him and his tail is lifted slightly and has a gentle curl. All of these pieces – from his nose to his tail including his posture – show a horse who is willingly moving forward towards something that has caught his interest.

High Headed with Hollow Back is a stressful and aggressive posture. This is the frame of a horse chasing off another horse. The horse's ears are usually pinned back, his nostrils flared and lips tight. His tail may be held tight showing he is feeling some fear or tension, stiffly out at an angle showing he is unsure, or swishing showing he is angry. In any case, his body is tense. If he charges at the other horse, his energy is strong. .If the horse takes this posture in a more playful way – as when young horses or geldings playfully compete with each other – the trail will be held very high or even straight up in the air, the ears will be forward, the face relaxed. In either situation, the horse's movement is more up and down than forward because his tense back prevents his hindquarters from reaching far underneath him. Because a horse in this frame is already stressed, tense or excited, he is more likely to react strongly to external stimuli – even to objects and situations that would normally not affect him.

The photo below and on the following page show the natural frame of High Headed with Hollow Back

Above: Compared with the photo on the previous page of 'high headed and level' posture, you can see that this horse's right hind leg does not reach very far under his body nor does his front right leg have much extension. His back is slightly more concave, his ears are back and the nose is more elevated

The horse in this photo is also in the High Headed with Hollow Back posture as he assertively pushing his herd mates away. Note the very elevated nose, pinned ears and squared upper lip.

Round Poll with Hollow Back is an unnatural frame created by the rider that creates physical and mental stress. The horse is over bent at the poll with his nose pulled well in behind the vertical (towards his chest). This frame restricts his breathing and creates tension in his neck that travels along the spine. The horse's weight falls more on his forehand and he is unable to step well underneath himself. Riding a horse in this frame creates chronic pain, emotional trauma and prevents the horse from performing at his best.

The photo below shows a horse being worked at the trot with a round poll and hollow back. His facial expression clearly shows his distress. The physical affect can be seen in his hindquarters which show little muscle development or roundness.

The Rest of the Picture

To fully and correctly interpret the body language of your horse, you must also pay attention to his eyes, muzzle (mouth & nostrils), ears, tail, energy, and muscle tension. Only by considering all these components together will you get the whole story.

Ears – Listening and Focus

Your horses ears combined with other body signals tell you where his attention is focused and what emotional state he is in. The ears are extremely mobile which allows him to swivel them 180 degrees to focus on

sounds coming for all directions. This is an essential trait for a prey animal that must be always vigilant for stealthy predators.

Although horses cannot hear low pitched sounds as well as humans can, he may be able to detect them as vibrations. They can, however, hear much higher pitched sounds than we do. Remember this the next time your horse reacts to something you can't hear. It is also important to realize that windy conditions distort sounds making them appear louder, difficult to identify or picked up from further distances. Since horses don't like uncertainty – they can't feel safe unless they know what or who is moving around them and exactly where it is – they are naturally unsettled on windy days.

What Ear Positions Mean:

The position of your horse's ears tells you where his attention is focused and whether he is alert or relaxed.

Pricked Sharply Forward ears show that a sound, movement or object in front of him has caught his attention.

Relaxed 'V' Shape ears indicate the horse is feeling relaxed but still focused. The horse will occasionally flick his ears giving momentary attention to something. He is focused without tension and still pay attention to what is going on around him.

Pointing Backwards ears mean that the horse is focused on something behind him or on his rider. When being ridden, it can sometimes be an indication that he is anxious or confused.

One Forward One Back indicates the horse's attention is taken in two directions. He may be listening to you talk to him while you're riding and paying attention to something ahead of him on the trail.

Pinned Back ears signal an angry horse. How far back the ears go indicates how annoyed or angry the horse is. A momentary ear pinning along with a head shake is a warning to move away. Ears pinned back so far that they seem to disappear into the horse's mane are a sign to take extreme caution as the horse is very angry and may bite, strike or kick.

Flopping to Sides ears held in this posture tell you the horse is extremely relaxed and content.

Eyes – Vision and Communication

Horses have the largest eyes (in relations to body size) of all the land mammals. These beautiful features allow the horse to have almost 360 degree vision with one blind spot directly in front of him that extends for out about 1 metre, and another directly behind him. He has binocular vision in  front and monocular vision on each side. So, he has a very different view of the world than we do. Remember that when your horse is worried about something that either you don't see (it might be behind you) or you don't find to be scary.

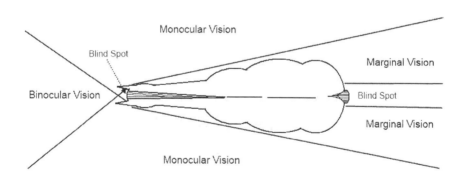

What the Eyes Tell You:

The eyes may be the windows to the soul, but they also provide some information about how your horse is feeling. Considering the horse's eyes in combination with other signals from his body gives you a more clear interpretation of his mood.

Open and Soft eyes generally mean the horse is relaxed and calm.

Half Closed eyes on a quiet horse indicate the horse is resting and not paying attention. However, an angry horse may also have half closed eyes. Paying attention to clues from the rest of his body will give you a clear message. Take another look at the photos showing ears flopping to the sides and pinned back ears and you will notice that they both have half closed eyes.

Wide Open eyes that are intently focused in a particular direction or on a specific object tell you that something has caught the horse's attention. He may be curious or interested. If the whites are showing he is feeling high level of stess which may be fear, anxiety or anger. Note that some horses naturally have a white rim 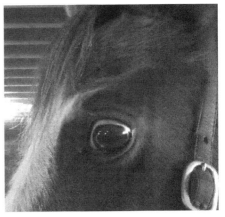 around the edge of their eye. Paying attention to clues from the rest of his body will give you a clear message.

Darting with Unfixed Focus show that the horse is feeling uncertain about a situation.

Muzzle – Nostrils, Mouth and Chin

The horse's muzzle includes his nostrils, mouth and chin. It is much more sensitive than the human hand. It has more nerve ending per square centimeter than our fingers. It's mobility makes it very useful for sorting through food sources. Even the whiskers have an important 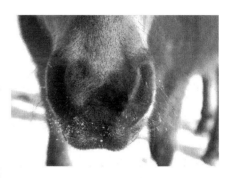 function of investigating by touch where the horse can't see (remember that blind sport directly in front of him).

The muscles in the jaw and mouth affect the suppleness of the poll. Tension from a locked jaw can be transferred to the rest of the body and vice versa.

What the Muzzle Tells You:

Relaxed nostrils & muzzle indicates calmness and relaxation.

Flared Nostrils can indicate alertness due to alarm or fright (especially if combined with snorting) or checking out an unusual or strong scent. It can also be the result of heavy exercise.

Pinched Nostrils show the horse is feeling pain or is angry.

Wrinkled nostrils & muzzle means the horse is nervous or worried.

Upper Lip Protruding signals that the horse is enjoying something you are doing to his body like scratching his withers or grooming a particularly itchy spot. The more the lip protrudes – and even wiggles – the more your horse is enjoying that scratch or grooming.

Horses also use their strong upper lip to check out things and move them. Some horses will push with their upper lip instead of biting.

Tight Lips signify anxiety, tension, nervousness.

Drooping lower lip shows relaxation. It is often seen in horses that are dozing. It is a sure sign that your horse is very comfortable.

Flapping lower lip is a sign of tension, nervousness, being distracted or worried.

Licking and Chewing indicates a change in state and usually happens as the horse relaxes after (or gets relief from) a situation where he felt stressed or threatened

.Open mouth 'snapping' is most often seen in foals and is a submissive gesture indicating "I'm a baby please don't hurt me".

Yawning can be a calming or appeasement signal that usually happens as the horse is starting to feel stressed and is trying to calm himself down or following a stressful situation and he is releasing tension.

Tail – More Than Pest Control

The horse's tail has only two purposes - protection and communication. Besides being a highly effective fly swatter, it also provides cover for the anus and urethra as well as a barrier to the elements.

Because it is an extension of his spine, the horse's tail is affected by tension along the spinal column. Keep in mind that how the horse carries his tail can be an indication of pain, crookedness or muscle tension in the hindquarters or back.

What the Tail Tells You:

As part of the horse's body language, the tail can express at least six different messages.

Softly Curled means the horse is feeling calm and comfortable. The horse's conformation and breed affects the height at which a horse normally carries his tail. For example, Arabians tend to naturally carry their tails higher than Quarter Horses.

Swishing signals that the horse is irritated, resistant, annoyed or in pain. The energy in the swish indicates the amount of annoyance from mild to severe. (photo on next page)

Wringing or Twirling indicates the horse is very resistant, angry, aggressive or in pain.

Sticking Straight Out or Up shows the horse is excited, competitive and aroused in some way. A very high tail means the horse is in 'high spirits' and playful.

Stiffly Held Out at an Angle expresses the horse's apprehension about a situation.

Clamped tail is a sign of submission, tiredness, not feeling well or fear. The tighter the tail is tucked in to the hindquarters, the more fearful the horse is feeling.

The photos below are both of Quarter Horses. The first photo shows a **softly curled tail.**

The photo below shows a **tail held out stiffly at an angle.**

In the 3 following photos, the horse on the left is **twirling** her tail in anger as the rider pulls on the reins to try to rebalance herself; the horse on the right is **swishing** her tail to the right side in annoyance at the spur being used on her side; the race horse in the bottom photo has his tail **sticking straight out** in excitement.

Photo credit: Jackie Timmings

Photo credit: Jade Krafsig

Reading the Whole Body From Nose to Tail

To get a better understanding of the horse's message, read the whole body from muzzle to tail.

In the photo above, the horse on the left shows passive body language. The horse on the right shows aggression with his ears flat back, mouth ready to bite, and a bit of white visible in the inside corner of his eye.

These two horses are focused on something in the distance. While their heads are up and their ears are pricked forward, their square front legs and soft tails indicate that they are not alarmed. They have "attention without tension" as they have simply heard a noise or seen a movement that they need to check out. If the source is located and deemed to be non-threatening, they will resume grazing or dozing. If they can't determine the source or

it is deemed to be a potential threat, they will 'high tail' it away to put some distance between themselves and the perceived threat.

Your body language also affects how your horse feels. In this photo, the woman is enjoying 'face time' with her horse. Her posture is very common for us. As she looks up at her horse's eyes, her core energy is sent upwards into his head/neck. The horse lifts his head or moves it to the side, but the human holds it centred. This horse shows some tension in his mouth as he pushes out his upper lip and

Core energy pushing into horse's head/neck. Sends his head up.

his ears are slightly back. He is probably trying to push the woman away with his head. This is his polite way of asking her to get out of his face. Compare this interaction with the next photo.

This woman is in a more horse friendly posture that brings her 'nose to nose' with her horse. She has brought herself lower than the horse (no core energy directed at his head) which encourages the horse to lower his head. The horse's muzzle and eye are both soft.

Developing More Awareness - Grooming

Grooming is a good place to being developing more awareness for reading your horse's body language and changing how he feels. What happens while you groom your horse affects the tone for the rest of the time you spend together. Too often grooming is done quickly and without paying any real attention to the horse.

If your horse won't stand still in the cross-ties, pins his ears, swishes his tail or tries to bite or kick, he is feeling anxious and tense. By changing how you look at grooming, you can help your horse develop more trust, be more relaxed and become more cooperative.

When it comes right down to it, grooming is ground work. Just like every other aspect of training, it should focus on helping your horse feel calmer and more relaxed whenever he is with you - even when he is away from his herd mates. Grooming is also a natural behaviour for horses even in the wild. Strong bonds are formed between two horses who mutually groom each other. You see them scratch each backs and withers. This behaviour also reduces social anxiety. The bonded horses have developed enough mutual trust that they relax their personal space boundaries knowing that there is no threat to their safety. When your grooming sessions simulate this natural herd behaviour, you can create a similar bond with your horse.

Steps for Quality Grooming:

Set the mood for your quality grooming time. Take your horse to a safe, quiet area where distractions for both of you are minimized. Focus your attention on your horse and save human socializing for later. If your horse has separation anxiety, minimize his stress by having your session where he can still see his 0he0rd mates or special buddy. Having your grooming session after your horse has been exercised can also help minimize excess energy or anxiety.

Encourage a calm, relaxed frame of body. Whether you use either cross ties or a single tie, ensure he is able to comfortably have his neck level (poll level with withers). When his poll is higher than his withers, adrenaline is turned on, his back drops and he feels physically and mentally tense. Ask him to stand with his front feet square rather than scissored (split). When the front feet are scissored, he is ready to move. Standing square puts him mentally and physically in "park".

Be aware of your horse's whole body – from nose to tail. Standing near his shoulder keeps you safe & gives you full view of his body. You need to notice even subtle signals that tell you how he is feeling and to pro-actively stop unwanted behaviour. If he steps, bends or shifts his weight towards you, he is pushing into your personal space. Stop whatever you are doing. Ask him to stay out of your space by blocking or pushing away the offending body part. For example, if he leans his shoulder into you or steps his front foot toward you block or push that shoulder until he shifts his weight or moves his foot away. If he bends into you, block or push his barrel near his girth until he straightens or bends away from you. This response tells him to respect your personal space. (See Chapter 6 – Boundaries – With All Due Respect)

When your horse has yielded to your block or push, reward him with a wither scratch then continue grooming. If your horse has learned to push people or has a lot of anxiety, you may initially spend more time changing his posture and pushiness than grooming. It may take a few sessions, but is well worth the effort. With consistency and calmness his behaviour will improve.

Be aware of your own body language, energy and alignment to your horse. Horses respond to pushing, blocking and drawing energy from our hips, shoulders, arms and core. He reads your movements and energy the same way he reads other horses.

If your horse respects you enough to step away when you ask by pointing at or pushing his hip, he will do so even if you inadvertently push towards it. He doesn't know that you didn't mean it. If some part of your body pushes towards the vulnerable areas of his neck or head, he will feel threatened. A passive horse will turn his head away from you causing his shoulder to push into you. An assertive horse will give you a bump with his head or bite you. An aggressive horse might strike or kick you. Punishing your horse for behaviours you inadvertently cause creates anxiety, conflict and resentment.

Make a connection to your horse's body through touch. Using gentle pressure with the flat of your hand, stroke over his entire body – head to tail and back to feet. Use your hand furthest from his head to avoid pushing into his personal space (i.e. on his left side, use your right arm; on his right side, use your left arm). Notice any areas where he is ticklish, reactive or moves away. Also notice any sore spots, cuts, bumps, or hot or cold areas that can be a sign of inflammation or poor circulation. Palpate both sides of his spine from withers to croup and notice any sensitive areas which could be signs of poor saddle fit or a need for massage or chiropractic therapy.

Treat your horse's skin gently. Horses do not have elephant skin. It is sensitive enough to feel a fly land on it. Save your hard metal or rubber curry for cleaning your other brushes. Use a soft rubber curry to remove dried sweat and dirt. For really sensitive horses or areas, a "scrubby" sponge may be a better alternative. To remove loose dirt and hair, brushes with natural hair bristles are gentler than hard, synthetic bristles, and naturally polish the hair. Try the brushes on your own arm or face to feel the difference. A sheepskin mitt, a wool sock over your hand or a soft cloth is good for very sensitive areas on the body as well as on the face. A very soft brush (goat hair is great) is also nice on the face.

Quality grooming is a massage. When using the curry, a mitt or cloth, move your hand in circles with gentle pressure. Take your time and let your horse enjoy the experience. Experiment with the amount of pressure your horse likes in different areas and with different types of brushes. Pay attention to his behaviour so you will know whether or not he is enjoying it. He may show pleasure by leaning into your brush, moving his lips or even trying to reach around to reciprocate the grooming. Do not punish him for returning the favour by yelling at him, hitting him or pushing his head away. If you are paying attention, you will notice his intention and can quietly without aggression block him from coming into your space with your flat hand or the bristles of the brush. If your horse gets upset, stop what you are doing, bring him back to a calm frame and protect your personal space. Start grooming again in an area he enjoyed then gradually move back to the sensitive area. Adjust your pressure or try a different grooming tool.

The series of photos on the following pages shows how reshaping a horse's posture while grooming her changes how she feels about the experience. The horse in the photos is a very sensitive Arabian mare who did not like to be touched, groomed or tacked up. She would 'dance' in the cross ties. In her stall, she would pin back her ears, threaten to bite and turn her hind quarters towards the person in her stall. Her body language was used as a warning and a threat. She had never bitten or kicked anyone. However, when this type of body language is given, the possibility of the follow through action is always present.

The photos show how I was able to change her behaviour (frame of mind) by changing her posture (frame of body) and by changing my own body language while working with her.

141

Body Language While Grooming

1. The mare's body language - high head, pinned ears, flared nostrils - shows her displeasure with how I am grooming her. She is leaning into me with her left shoulder. I have caused this behaviour by brushing her with my left arm which sends impulsive (pushing) energy into her head and neck (the "no go zone").

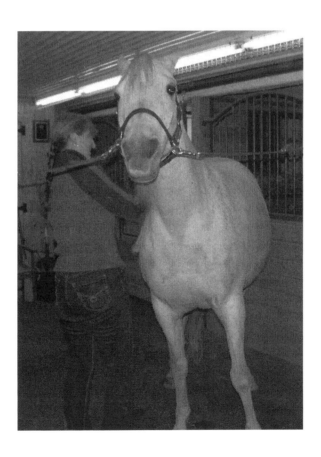

2. In the next two photos, I have taken the mare off the cross ties so I can reshape her posture. Massaging her girth button encourages her to move her barrel away from me and come into a deeper bend. As she comes into this "feel good" shape, she lowers her neck and relaxes her back. I have adjusted my posture so that my open right hip invites her to bring her nose there.

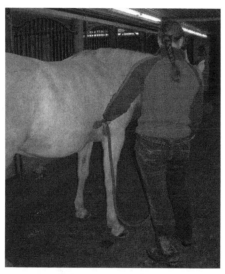

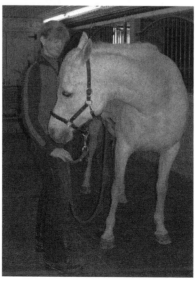

3. The final photo shows the mare's body language is now relaxed, level and calm. Her poll is level with her withers. She is bent around me rather than pushing into me. She is standing square with her front feet. When your horse is in this "feel good" posture, she can enjoy her grooming session and her time with you.

Grooming is an opportunity to develop a positive relationship with your horse based on mutual trust and respect. When you pay attention to your horse's feedback, you know what areas he enjoys having groomed and can identify areas that are sensitive, uncomfortable or sore. How you groom sets the mood for your riding or ground work session. When it is a mutually pleasurable experience, you both reap the benefits.

It takes awareness and practice to notice, interpret and understand all the pieces of your horse's body language. Start with the basics of good feeling and bad feeling postures. Then when your horse is stressed, you can help him feel calm and more confident by encouraging him to come into a calm shape. The next section provides more information and practical exercises to apply these techniques with your horse.

Part 3

DEVELOPING PARTNERSHIP IN THE SADDLE

"Anything forced and misunderstood can never be beautiful.
And to quote the words of Simon: If a dancer was forced to
dance by whip and spikes, he would be no more beautiful than
a horse trained under similar conditions.

~ Xenophon 400 BC

Chapter 9 – Balance, Posture & Confidence

If you are like most adult riders, you want to have a calm, well balanced, respectful and willing partnership with your horse – especially when you're riding him. The good news is that your horse wants and needs the same thing.

Riding is much like ballroom dancing. When it works well, there is a subtle communication and connection between the partners that creates seemingly effortless and flowing movements. Each partner influences the frame and movement of the other.

One partner leads the dance giving subtle cues through their body which the other partner fluidly responds to and follows. The two move as one as they send and receive information through their bodies to each other. The foundation of this connection is the body posture or frame of each partner. The elements of a good frame are alignment, balance and suppleness combined with strength. It is these elements that allow the partners to feel each other without interfering with the movement of each other. A lack of even one of these elements will cause the connection to break down resulting in stiff, uncoordinated and ungraceful movements.

Imagine yourself dancing the waltz with 2 different partners. The first partner is tense and holds you stiffly without any suppleness or rhythm. You feel unbalanced and slightly anxious as you step on each other's feet and bump into other dancers. You might even try to take the lead yourself. The second partner is relaxed and confident. He supports you in a strong, but supple frame and gently guides you as you glide around the floor. You feel comfortable and confident. Now, change the picture to the riding arena where you and your horse are the dance partners. Which dance partner are you? To be able to perform at his best, your horse needs you to be like the second partner – balanced, supple and relaxed.

Ideally, you are the leader of the dance with your horse. To achieve this relationship, you need to develop a balanced, supple and strong posture without being stiff, rigid or, at the other extreme, a ragdoll. A quiet, stable body that moves fluidly maximizes the amount of useful information that can be transmitted from you to your horse's body. A busy, unbalanced body becomes rigid and creates interference by making it difficult – if not impossible – for the horse to understand or feel your cues.

In the same way, it is difficult for you to ride a horse comfortably whose body is stiff and rigid with tension. When the mind is anxious or fearful it is difficult to have a relaxed, supple body. It also is not easy to have a positive frame of mind when your body is tense.

When you are in the saddle, the most important factor that affects how your horse feels is how you are sitting on him. You are sitting on the back of an animal that is not designed to carry a rider. And, you are sitting on the spinal column which, as part of the central nervous system, sends sensory messages to your horse's brain. So, how you sit directly affects how your horse feels both physically and mentally. He needs to be able to carry himself in a healthy posture and develop strength in the correct muscles in order to perform at his best without causing pain or damage to his body. To do this, your horse must be able to reach his hind feet well underneath himself so that he lifts his back and carries himself with his hindquarters.

Your horse is very aware of and affected by your balance, your alignment (both vertically and to the horse) and the suppleness or stiffness of your body. If you are unbalanced, tense or out of alignment, then you will be fixing what you are causing in the horse.

Balance and Confidence

Balance and confidence are linked for both you and your horse. Just think of how uncomfortable you feel when you are in a situation where you think you might fall. How about the first few times you tried downhill skiing, ice skating or riding a bicycle? You feel emotionally 'insecure' when you have an insecure seat on your horse. There's that mental/physical connection again.

When you are off balance, your brain thinks you are in danger and automatically triggers your fear responses - tension and gripping in your muscles and joints, shallow breathing, etc. Of course, your horse feels this tension and bracing from you which affects how he feels.

Even if your horse is such a steady eddie that he doesn't get too flustered by the tension in your body, his balance will be thrown off, too. When you are off-balance, you will not be able to follow your horse's motion or give him clear cues for what you want him to do. You will try to maintain your balance by hanging on to the reins and pushing into the stirrups. You may end up:

- Falling behind your horse's motion,

- leaning too far forward,

- leaning off to one side, or

- shifting your weight onto the wrong seat bone.

How horses react to these uncomfortable feelings depends on their age, experience, and temperament. Generally, they try to resolve it in one of several ways:

- running away be speeding up or scooting forward

- slowing down or stopping

- turning or drifting when the rider wants to go straight

- falling in or out of the turn

- going in a different direction than the rider wanted.

You and your horse are reflections of each other – mentally and physically. So, you may be inadvertently contributing to your horse's stress and imbalance which causes training issues such as:

- rushed transitions,

- falling on the forehand,

- pulling against the reins,

- cross cantering,

- spooking,

- bucking.

Of course, these types of training issues contribute to your stress and lack of confidence and can cause you to be tense and out of balance as well. It's a vicious cycle.

Balance is the foundation of good riding and is reciprocal between horse and rider. It is difficult for one partner to be balanced if the other is not. In both horse and rider, loss of balance causes stress, tension and resistance. Older, well schooled horses can compensate to some extent for the rider's imbalance with minimal effect on performance. The same is true of balanced, supple experienced riders on young, green and unbalanced horses. However, neither horses nor riders who have little experience, who are sensitive or nervous can cope with an unbalanced partner.

It requires a solid foundation from one partner to not only compensate for, but also help the other partner find and maintain balance so that the two become equal partners. What we want from the horse, we must first be able to give to the horse. To have soft, supple and balanced horses, we must be soft, supple and balanced riders.

Relaxation and Suppleness

When you are off balance, your body will do its best to keep you safe by tensing your muscles and joints in an attempt to hang on to the saddle. Tension in one part of your body will transfer to other areas. To experience how this works, tense the fingers in your right hand. Now try moving your shoulder forwards, backwards and up and down. Now release the tension from your hand and move your shoulder again in the same ways. Did you notice that your shoulder did not move as freely when your fingers were tense? The tension traveled from your fingers through your hand, wrist, lower arm, elbow, upper arm and shoulder. You may have also noticed that it traveled into your neck and down your back.

When you hold tension in your body, your muscles and joints are stiff, you will be unable to move with your horse and you will lose your alignment to your horse. It takes practice and awareness to recognize where you hold tension, when it creeps in and how you release it.

Like many adult riders, you may carry tension in your body without realizing it is there. Our bodies store the stress we take on during our daily lives. Before you get on your horse and after you get in the saddle, do a body scan and notice where you are holding tension. I have made this a regular part of my routine and it makes a big difference to how I feel when I'm riding. The more you practice it, the easier and more unconscious it becomes. If a horse I'm riding spooks, I can usually release my own burst of adrenaline and tension quickly. I used to have to get off the horse and de-stress myself from the ground before continuing my ride. But, now I can usually do it while staying on the horse.

To help improve your awareness for and ability to release tension, practice the Calm, Focused Breath and the Body Focus exercises described in Chapter 2. Scan your body from the top of your head and work your way down through the back of your neck, your shoulders, shoulder blades, arms, hands, spine, small of your back, buttocks, hips, thighs, knees, calves, ankles and toes.

Move and rotate any area where you notice the tension. While you are riding, periodically scan your body and release the tension that quietly sneaks back into those areas.

This is a good technique to practice even when you are not riding (eg. driving your car, sitting at a desk, etc.) If you carry tension in your body in your life generally, it will not magically disappear when you get on your horse.

Rider Posture and Alignment

Regardless of the type of riding you do, the ability to find balance, suppleness and relaxation for both you and your horse begins with the correct posture. Good posture requires the engagement of your core muscles to support your upper body without creating tension in your spine, hips or arms.

Your core muscles are located just below your belly button. If you aren't sure where these muscles are, stand or sit up straight and place your hand across your abdomen just below your belly button. Contract and expand the muscles you feel underneath your hand. You should still be able to breathe normally when these muscles are contracted. If your breathing is affected, you are tightening the muscles above your belly button and interfering with your diaphragm.

To find the correct posture on your horse, your seat bones should be pointing straight down towards the ground. Tip your pelvis slightly forwards so that your tail bone is tucked slightly under you. Tighten your core muscles and imagine your rib cage filling with helium so that it floats over your hips. Let your arms drop softly out of your shoulder sockets, dropping them away from your ears and relaxing your shoulder blades down your back. Continue to breathe using your diaphragm (calm, focused breath). Allow your legs to fall out of your hip sockets and to open slightly so that your knees and the front of your thighs are not gripping the saddle. Gently hug your horse's barrel with your calves while allowing your ankles to soften. Let your hip flexors and leg muscles lengthen as you allow your knees to drop away from your hips.

When you have the correct position and remain relaxed and supple, you will feel like your seat bones are plugged into your saddle, your hips will swing in a figure eight following the movement of your horse's barrel (swinging side to side) and hips (stepping forward). This movement is much the same as how your hips move when you walk. You can get a better feeling for this movement by riding with your eyes closed while someone you trust leads or lunges your horse.

Independent Seat

With this posture, you are now on your way to developing an independent seat that will allow you to ride with balance, suppleness, quiet hands and subtle aids. You will be lighter on your horse's back allowing him to move and carry himself with less effort as you work with and enhance your horse's natural movement and carriage.

With an independent seat, you can move each part of your body independently while maintaining suppleness and strength. You remain balanced over the horse's centre of gravity at all gaits without gripping or tilting. You will be more relaxed in the saddle and able to apply subtle, quiet aids through your seat bones, legs and even your breath that work with the natural function and structure (bio-mechanics) of your horse.

The foundation of an independent seat is alignment. There are three areas of alignment necessary for both you and your horse to be balanced and relaxed.

1. The spine – In the rider, this is the vertical alignment from the top of your head to your tail bone. It creates the straight line of "ear over shoulder over hip over heel". In your horse, this is the horizontal alignment from the nose to the tail.

2. The rectangle – This is the same for you and your horse. Your shoulders and hips create a box. Your shoulders should stay over your hips and your horse's hips should track directly behind his shoulders.

3. Horse and Rider - You and your horse should always have the same alignment. That means that your belly button aims between your horse's ears; your shoulders align with your horses shoulders; and, your hips align with your horse's hips.

Requirements for an Independent Seat

1. True vertical alignment - a straight line starting from your ear traveling through your shoulder and hip and ending at your heel.

2. A following seat that moves with the swing of the horse's barrel and hips. Your pelvis tips slightly forward so that your seat bones point down towards the ground (your tail bone is tucked slightly underneath you). The small of your back is flat (not arched) and supported by your engaged core muscles.

3. Your weight is evenly balanced over both seat bones and the back of your pubic bone.

4. Your core (belly button) is aimed between your horse's ears and follows the subtle bend in your horse's spine.

5. Your legs hang softly out of your hip sockets allowing the hip flexors to lengthen rather than contract. Your knees are soft and may fall slightly away from the saddle. Your toes turn out at a natural angle – no more than 45° from your horse's barrel.

6. Contact to your horse's mouth is maintained through the reins with soft, closed hands, flat wrists, elastic elbows and soft shoulders. Your arms hang softly out of the shoulder sockets with your upper arms dropped along the side your ribs and your elbows slightly in front of your mid-line.

Alignment for An Independent Seat

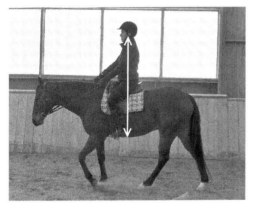

Rider's Vertical Alignment

Ear over shoulder over hip over heel

Rectangle

Shoulders and hips square

Horse and Rider

Belly button aims between horse's ears. Shoulders and hips aligned.

Common Posture Problems

Riders with poor posture are unbalanced and have tense muscles and locked joints. They grip with their legs or pinch with their knees and rely on the reins and stirrups for support. All of this tension interferes not only with the riders' ability to feel their horses' movement, but also with the horses' natural balance, alignment, rhythm and ability to move comfortably.

Here are some common posture problems:

1. Falling behind the vertical. If you have this posture, you are leaning back with your shoulders behind your hips. This causes your lower leg pushes forward as you brace into the stirrups (sometimes described as riding with your feet on the dash), your upper body becomes stiff as you try to balance yourself with your arms and the reins. Your horse will feel pulling or, at the very least, no release from the rein. You are 'behind the motion' of your horse's movement.

You have put the brakes on through your upper body while you have a driving seat causing the horse to hollow his back and raise is head.

In this inverted frame, your horse cannot engage his hindquarters or lift his back. This frame creates a release of adrenaline as well as physical stress to the spine and back muscles. Physically and mentally the horse is in flight mode, he is unbalanced and rushes forward with quick, short steps that lack suspension.

2. Falling forward. In this position, your shoulders are in front of the vertical line. Your weight is over your horse's shoulders making it more difficult for him to stay off the forehand, bring his hindquarters underneath himself or lift his back. In order to feel balanced, you will grip with your knees causing your lower leg to be insecure as they come off your horse's barrel or fall far behind the girth line. You cannot use your seat, leg or rein aids clearly or effectively.

In this position, the horse may feel pressure or pain in his shoulders and withers and going forward will be uncomfortable. He may be slow moving or refuse to move forward at all. He is also unresponsive or very slow to respond to your leg aids.

Again, your balance is compromised. You will not be able to maintain a supple, following seat or contact because your body will be tense.

3. Crooked in the saddle. In this position, your weight is more on one side than the other. This position can be caused by collapsing sideways at the waist (ribs drop towards hip), dropping one shoulder or letting one shoulder or hip be in front of the other one. You tend to hold more on one rein than the other which pulls your horse's nose to one side throwing him off balance. He also moves away from the side where he feels more of your weight. This position makes it very difficult for your horse to travel in a straight line or to turn into the side bearing more weight

Exercise: Improve Your Posture & Alignment

Your balance in the saddle is affected by your posture as well as your alignment with your horse. If you can, have your coach or another experienced rider take a close look at your position, your horse's straightness and your alignment to each other. If there are mirrors in your arena, you can check your posture occasionally while you are riding. Another option is to have someone video your ride and review it later. You should watch the video at least 3 times. The first 2 times you will probably be too critical of yourself. By the time you watch it the third time, you will be able to look for specific areas where you have room for improvement.

Do this exercise first at the walk and then at the trot.

Ride a straight line towards and away from the ground person, mirror or video camera.

Ride circles in both directions.

Check the three areas of alignment that are necessary for both you and your horse be balanced and relaxed:

1. Spine:
    a. You - the straight line from your "ear through your shoulder through your hip through your heel".

    b. Your Horse - the horizontal alignment from his nose to his tail.

2. Rectangle - the same for both horse & rider as the shoulders and hips create a box.
    a. You – your shoulders stay over your hips
    b. Your Horse – his hind feet track directly behind his front feet.

3. Horse and Rider – You and your horse should be aligned to each other.

    a. Your belly button aims between your horse's ears

    b. Your shoulders align with your horses shoulders;

    c. Your hips align with your horse's hips.

Exercise: Improve Your Balance with the Half Seat Position

Riding in the half seat position is a great way to improve your balance in the saddle. When done correctly, you have light contact with your lower leg and inner thigh with your seat just slightly lifted out of the saddle. There should not be any "daylight" visible between you and your saddle. You can stay in this position comfortably without requiring the support of your arms or gripping too tightly with your legs.

This exercise can be done on your own on a quiet, reliable horse in a safe environment. If your horse is more sensitive or reactive, it is best to enlist the help of your coach or other experienced horse person to hold, lead and/or lunge your horse while you do this exercise.

While your horse is standing still, go into your half seat by lifting your hip and pushing it slightly back towards the saddle's cantle. As you do this, your hip angle will close and your shoulders will become forward and lower. Initiate the movement from the hips not by dropping the shoulders forward. The shoulder position changes only as the hip angle closes. If there is daylight visible between your seat and the saddle, you are using your stirrups to support you and lifting yourself too far out of the saddle. At first, you may need to support yourself with your hands on your horse's neck or by holding a handful of mane so that you don't inadvertently pull on the reins. Once you feel balanced, gently lift your hands off your horse's neck while keeping a light contact on the reins. If you have someone holding your horse from the ground, you can put your arms out to the sides and level with your shoulders.

If you are having difficulty balancing, help your leg stay under you by pushing through your knee toward the ground the same way you would if you were squatting. Be careful to keep the weight in your heels or you may "goose" your horse to go forward. The entire leg must remain soft and supple while gently hugging the horse's barrel. Allow your knees to open and your toes to turn out naturally at about a 45 degree angle from the barrel. Pinching your knees in causes the lower leg to come off the barrel causing you to become a teeter totter. Breathe and release any tension in your body from the shoulders through the arms to the fingers and down through your spine all the way to your toes. Your hips, knees and ankle joints need to be soft and relaxed to act as shock absorbers.

Maintain your balance in the half seat position for a count of 10 then gently lower your seat back into the saddle being careful not to thump down on your horse's back or balance off the reins. When you have found your balance at halt, repeat the same exercise at walk and then trot. If your leg contact is steady and your rein contact is consistent, your horse should be able to relax, lengthen his spine, and move in a comfortable and consistent rhythm. You should be able to do transitions from 3 point to half seat without losing your balance or disturbing your horse's rhythm or frame.

When you have reached this stage, you can increase the challenge by taking the half seat position as your horse walks or trots over the centre of ground poles spaced about 3-4 feet apart. To develop more feel and awareness for his movement, count the number of steps your horse takes between each pole.

Feel the movement as he lifts his feet to step over the poles. If your horse slows down at the poles, push with your legs in time with the swing of his barrel – left leg as his barrel swings right, right leg as his barrel swings left – to encourage him to continue forward without losing momentum.

If he rushes at the poles, inhale deeply as you lift your shoulders up and back slightly and tighten your core. Be careful not to put tension in your whole body. On the next beat, exhale and release your shoulders slightly. This creates a half halt effect which you can repeat until your horse responds.

By developing a balanced, supple and independent seat, you will be the better dance partner helping your horse perform to his best without resistance or stress.

A lovely half seat position at the trot. The rider in the photo above is nicely balanced over the centre of her saddle. Notice how much her leg has lengthened as she now has weight in her knee and ankle. She now has a much more solid and effective foundation.

Correct Half Seat Position with the hips just lifted up and pushing back slightly with no daylight between the rider and the saddle. The inner thigh muscles are doing the work to support the rider in this position.

"One of the most fundamental rules of equitation is: straighten your horse and ride him forward."

~ Alois Podharsky

Chapter 10 – Working With (Not Against) Your Horse

With your own frame aligned, relaxed and balanced, you can now focus on helping your horse maintain a frame where he will also be balanced, able to move forward, engage his hindquarters and lift his back. Just like you, if your horse is not straight, he will be unbalanced, tense and unable to perform to his best ability. Of course, if this happens, it will do nothing to help build your mutual trust or confidence. You and your horse end up in a cycle of tension, resistance and fear. It is much easier to build confidence and trust in each other when you both feel balanced, calm and relaxed.

Your horse is correctly aligned when his spine is straight from nose to tail. His nose is in line with the centre of his chest, his neck is between his shoulders, his hind feet track directly behind his front feet and his spine mirrors the line he is traveling.

This alignment must be true whether you and your horse are traveling on a straight line or a curved line (e.g. a turn or a circle). When his hind feet track exactly in line with his front feet, if you were watching him from the ground as he comes straight towards or away from you, you would only see two of his legs. His front legs as he comes towards you and his back legs as he goes away. If you can see more than two legs, then the horse is not straight. When the horse is traveling the arc of a turn or a circle, the bend in his spine from poll to tail should be exactly over top of the arc.

Like us, horses don't carry themselves perfectly straight on their own. They have asymmetry in their bodies just as we do. When a horse is crooked over a period of time, he will develop soreness because one hind leg is always carrying more weight. The discomfort from the sore muscles or joints will be displayed by behaviours such as resistance to going forwards or in a certain direction, throwing his head, lameness or unevenness in his gaits, bucking, rearing or bolting.

So, while you work on keeping your own straightness and alignment in the saddle, it's also important that you are aware of and help your horse with his. You need to ride every step and make small corrections as needed. It's really much like driving a car. If you don't make small adjustments on the steering wheel and the gas pedal, you'll end drifting across the dividing line, into the ditch or hitting the car in front of you. Most of the time the adjustments you make a very subtle and done subconsciously. Eventually, it will become the same for you and your horse.

Aiding Your Horse to Straightness

You have 3 natural aids to communicate your instructions to your horse from your body to his:

- Seat – both seat bones and the movement of your hips

- Legs – lower leg (calf) and upper leg (thigh)

- Hands – the connection from the bit through the reins through your hands, wrists arms and into your shoulder blades.

Seat and Leg Aids

With your seat and legs, you can use the same 3 energies that were explained in Chapter 5 (Trust Builds Confidence) - driving (pushing), restraining (blocking) or following (drawing) - to influence the hindquarters, barrel and forequarters of your horse. You can block unwanted forward movement by slowing or stopping the movement in your hips. You can increase your horse's movement by increasing the movement of your hips. Your lower leg just behind the saddle girth or cinch creates bend. When moved back slightly, it influences your horse's hips. Your upper leg closes to block or push the horse's shoulder on the same side or opens to allow the horse to move his front end over.

Your legs and seat influence the horse's forward and lateral movement by communicating with the barrel, the hind legs and the front legs. Your leg aid, asks your horse to perform seven different actions:

1. go forward at walk, trot or canter

2. back up

3. turn on the haunches

4. turn on the forehand

5. leg yield

6. side pass

7. halt

Your left and right leg, your upper and lower leg, and your seat (seat bones and hips) all work independently of but in conjunction with each other. How you apply your individual leg and seat aids combined with your rein aids tells your horse which of the 7 movements to perform.

Reins Create Boundaries

Your hands through your reins can only apply 2 of the energies - restraining (blocking) or following (drawing). It's impossible for the reins to push your horse and they should never be used to pull your horse's head.

You keep your horse straight by using your reins as boundaries that keep his nose in line with the centre of his chest. If one hand is stronger than the other or your shoulders are crooked, you will pull your horse's nose off centre. Your reins create boundaries that tell your horse where not to go. The left rein prevents the horse's nose from turning right. The right rein prevents it from turning left. If you have uneven contact on your reins or are crooked in your shoulders, your horse can over bend through his neck.

To help keep your horse straight, keep your hands level with each other as if connected to a straight bar across your horse's withers. Your hands can move in and out on the bar to create open or direct rein aids, but they can't move up, down, backwards or forwards.

Photo Credit: Keith Timmings

170

Your reins will open or close 'doors'. Given a choice between an open and a closed door, you probably choose the open door. It's the easiest option. Your horse will make the same choice. To turn right, open your right rein like you're opening a door. Picture that straight bar extending out from your horse's withers and move your hand out (not back) to the side while keeping contact on the rein. Create a boundary with your outside rein by keeping your left hand on that imaginary bar closer to your horse's withers. Don't allow your left hand to move forward at all. Use your outside seat and leg aids in time with your horse's movement to firmly but gently guide him into the open right door.

When a rider uses the reins to steer her horse, she causes him to be crooked, throwing him off balance and creating resistance. You have probably seen (or perhaps experienced yourself) a situation where the rider attempts to steer her horse by pulling harder and harder one rein. In some cases, the rider may even bring her hand back behind her leg, bring her opposite hand across her horse's neck or do both. When this happens, the horse has both reins pulling him in opposite directions. (To experience how this feels, hold the bit in your hands while a friend pulls both reins in one direction.) At the same time, the rider might kick or spur her horse or apply the whip. All this activity causes the horse to become more tense, stressed and resistant. The more the rider pulls on the reins, the more she loses her own alignment, the more tense her body gets, the more her horse is bent out of shape, and the more he resists and pushes against her. Until the rider helps the horse become straight, it is very difficult for the horse to do what she is asking. If the rider releases the pressure on the pulling rein, corrects her own alignment and uses her leg and seat aids to square up the horse's hips and shoulders, the horse's resistance will decrease and he is more likely to be willing and able to do as the rider is asking.

The photographs on the following page show what happens when the horse and rider are crooked. Both riders are asking their horses to turn left. The rider in the photo on the top has over rotated her shoulders so that her right shoulder and hand are in front of her left. As a result, her left hand is coming back over her left leg. The rider in the photo below has collapsed her left hip. Notice that her left shoulder is lower than her right. In both cases, the rider has created misalignment in the rectangle of their hips/shoulders and their horses are mirroring their crookedness. Each horse's nose is pulled off the centre line and the right shoulder is bulging out of the turn. This shape causes the horse to drift out of the turn through his bulging shoulder.

It is common when this happens for the rider to try to fix the problem by pushing (or kicking) hard with the right leg and also pull on the left rein. Because the horse is now off balance as well as being pulled, he becomes tense in his jaw, neck and back and is unable to comfortably make the turn the rider is asking of him. As she feels the horse 'disobeying' and resisting what she wants, the rider also may become more tense, crooked and off balance. The rider ends up trying to fix a problem that she has created.

The two photos on the following page show examples of riders who have lost their alignment and how it affects their horses.

This rider's shoulders are crooked (right shoulder in front of her left) and she is pulling her horse's nose into the turn. The horse is over flexed through his neck. Both horse and rider are out of alignment (not straight) and off balance.

Photo Credit: Keith Timmings

This rider has collapsed her left hip – notice her left shoulder is lower than her right. Her horse will drift out of the turn (to the right) because his shoulders will be crooked as well. The horse mirrors the rider's alignment.

173

Bend is Your Friend

'True bend' and 'counter bend' are terms used to describe the horse's bend relative to the direction he is traveling. True bend means the horse is bent in the direction he is traveling. So, if you are walking on the left rein (counter clockwise) and your horse is bending around your left leg so that his spine is mirroring the line you are walking, then he is in true bend. If he is bending around your right leg when you are on the left rein, then his is in counter bend. In order to help her horse feel balanced, calm, supple and relaxed, it is important to be able to read which bend he has at any given moment.

Do not assume that because you are going to the left your horse has a left bend. This is the number one cause of misalignment between horse and rider. Practise reading your horse's bend by looking at his neck from the withers to his ears. Keep your belly button aimed between his ears so that your spine and his spine are always aligned to each other. At the rising trot, adjust your post so that you are rising as your horse's outside shoulder is going forward - that is the shoulder that is on the outside of his bend not the shoulder closest to the rail. You may have been taught to "rise and fall with the leg on the wall" – meaning that you rise as the shoulder closest to the rail is going forward. However, this teaching assumes that the horse has a true bend.

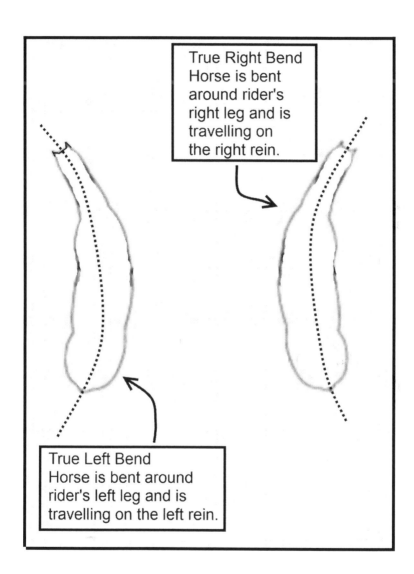

True Right Bend
Horse is bent
around rider's
right leg and is
travelling on
the right rein.

True Left Bend
Horse is bent around
rider's left leg and is
travelling on the left rein.

Bend and balance are fundamental to a horse's sense of security and safety. Horses use bend in two ways:

1. To protect them from perceived as well as real danger. By bending his body away from the potential threat he can quickly move away from the danger. This is why most horses want to bend away (counter bend) from the wall or corner when you are riding in the 'scary' end of the arena.

2. To communicate in the herd. One horse bending into another horse is a challenge and a signal to move out of the way. The first horse is pushing into the second horse's space. A lower ranking horse will bend away and yield the space to the higher ranking horse.

When you understand the importance of bend from the horse's perspective, you can see why giving up control of their bend is a big deal to many of them. When you have earned enough trust and respect to be seen by your horse as his worthy leader, and he does not feel like you are pushing him into a potentially dangerous place (that scary end of the arena again) then he will more readily change his bend when you ask.

But, it is also important that you know when to ask and which bend to ask for. You may have this experience that is common to many riders –the challenge of riding quietly in true bend through the spooky end of the arena or by the big rock (or some other object) on the trail. If you insist that your horse go into that corner or close to that rock by using more of what you think of as the "inside" leg, he feels like he is being trapped and pushed into a potentially dangerous and possibly life threatening situation. The result is more stress, imbalance and resistance.

The first step to be able to control your horse's bend is to be able to read his bend. To begin with you are going to work with whichever bend the horse is in at the time. Riding this way is for the short term only. You will not be concerned so much about where you go, but will focus on 'how you go'. That means you are focusing on keeping your feeling calm and relaxed by helping him stay in a level frame while also ensuring he is aligned nose to tail. This is easiest to do if you stay off the rail and work in the middle of the arena.

For example, you are traveling on the right rein, but the horse counter bends to the left. If you ask a horse to turn right when he is in left bend causes stress in his body. With the left bend, the horse can only comfortably leg yield to the right or turn left. Remember that you are focusing on keeping your horse balanced, comfortable and relaxed. So, rather than insisting the horse change his bend you use the counter bend to leg yield or change your mind about going right and make a turn to the left. This exercise requires you to tune into the horse and follow his bend. You temporarily give up asking for control of the bend in order to gain the horse's trust by keeping him in a relaxed and calm frame. Once the horse is staying in a level frame and is feeling calm, then you can ask him to change his bend and go past the 'scary' thing in true bend.

Some trainers and riders might think that this technique is "giving in to the horse" or "letting him win". But, really the horse does not know what we have planned to do. They don't know when we are going to ask them to turn right or left, do a leg yield, canter, go to a jump or circle away from the jump. All they know is whether or not what we are doing is making them feel relaxed or stressed. By working with the horse's bend instead of against it, you are enhancing the physiological benefits of smooth, balanced motion. As the horse feels physically more balanced, his levels of fear and stress are decreased. As you aid rather than dominate the horse, you earn the horse's trust and respect and the emotional authority to be his leader.

In order to turn and remain balanced, your horse's bend must match the arc of the turn. A stiff, unbending horse's hind quarters will swing out. If he is over bent (sometimes also called over flexed) through the neck, his shoulders will fall into the turn if his nose is tipped out of the turn or they will push out if his nose is tipped into the turn. A counter bent horse will be unbalanced.

When talking about 'inside' and 'outside' aids I am referring to them relative to the horse's bend. So, regardless of the direction you are traveling, the inside leg and inside rein are on the inside of the bend. The outside leg and outside rein on are on the outside of the bend. If your horse is bending right, your right leg and rein are the inside aids; your left leg and rein are the outside aids. When bending left, your left leg and rein are the inside aids; your right leg and rein are the outside aids.

Encourage your horse to bend around your inside seat bone and leg by keeping your leg just behind the girth or cinch of your saddle. Push his barrel over as you feel your inside hip drop. Help your horse to keep his hip in line by putting your outside leg back slightly and pushing his hip over when you feel your outside hip drop. If the inside shoulder is dropping in, push it over by using your upper inside leg as your horse's shoulder moves forward. The horse can only respond to your push when his weight is off the leg you want him to move.

It is easiest for your horse to change his bend when he is in a level or low frame. It is harder and causes more stress on his spine to change his bend when he is in an inverted frame (high headed with dropped back). You can help your horse to come out of an inverted frame by encouraging him to bend more into the bend he already has. Once he comes into a level frame, you can ask him to change his bend without causing additional stress.

When working on improving your horse's bend from your seat and leg aids, recognize when he tries a little. Stop pushing him and reward him with a wither scratch and a short break before asking again. Remember to reward yourself as well for a job well done.

Timing – There is a Right and a Wrong Time

Sometimes it can feel as if your horse is just ignoring you or intentionally doing the opposite of what you're asking him to do. The problem may simply be that you are asking him with the correct aid but at the wrong time. How you're asking (the aids you use) is only one part of the communication between you and your horse. The other very important part applying your aids at the moment your horse is able to respond to them. There really is a right time and a wrong time to ask your horse for a movement. To understand the importance of timing, you need to understand how your horse's body moves – the bio-mechanics of his movement.

Your horse's engine is in the rear. So, steering him is much like steering a boat. Whether it's the engine on a motor boat, the rudder on a sail boat or the paddle in a canoe, the direction the boat goes is determined from the back end. Trying to steer your horse by pulling his front end around with the reins simply throws him off balance, pulls him out of alignment and creates resistance.

As your horse moves: The hind legs push the horse forward.

1. The energy created travels diagonally through your horse's body (from left hip to right shoulder; from right hip to left shoulder).

2. The barrel swings out of the way of each hind leg – alternating left and right swing.

3. The head and neck swing over the front legs.

Picture your horse walking. Since his movement starts in the hind end, we'll follow the movement from back to front. As the left hind leg comes forward, the barrel swings out of its way by moving to the right. As the right front leg steps forward, the head and neck swing to the right. The right hind leg then comes forward sending the barrel over to the left. Then finally the left hind leg comes forward and the head and neck swing to the left. When your horse is relaxed and walking with a level neck, his back will swing and you will feel this movement through your seat and hips when you are also supple and relaxed.

How Your Horse Moves

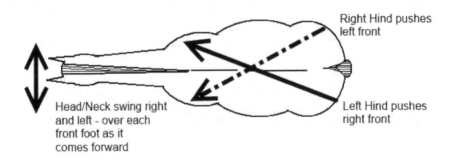

Right Hind pushes left front

Head/Neck swing right and left - over each front foot as it comes forward

Left Hind pushes right front

Since you can't see what is behind you, it's important to practice feeling the movement of your horse's hips to know where his hindquarters are. You can do this by closing your eyes for a few steps while at the walk. Have a trusted person lead or lunge you if it is not safe to do this on your own.

Now let's look at what happens when you want your horse to turn left. You have his body properly aligned and you are sitting square and balanced on his back. But, no matter how hard you push (or kick) with your left leg he just won't bend. If you are pushing when his barrel is swinging to the left, then you are just wasting energy and creating frustration for both of you. It is physically impossible for him to move his barrel to the right when it is swinging to the left. For your aid to be effective, you must push when your horse's barrel is swinging to the right. This is the moment when your left hip will be dropping and your right hip will be rising with the movement of the swinging barrel.

The right time to apply your aids always works with your horse's natural movement. Pushing on a shoulder or hip when that leg is on the ground or asking him to bend around your left leg when his barrel is swinging to the left is a waste of energy for you and a cause of confusion for your horse.

Some Common Training Problems and Solutions

1. Up Transitions

Problem: Your horse resists your cue to go forward by hollowing his back, flipping his head or backing up.

Reason: He may be feeling blocked from going forward. This can happen if you have inadvertently locked your hips and/or arms. If you are pushing hard from your seat or kicking with your legs, your body tends to tense and stiffen and you don't follow your horse's movement with your seat or reins. As a result, your horse feels blocked in the front end. He's not able to engage his hindquarters and lift his back so he can't comfortably move forward. Instead, he pushes against the rein (inverting his back and raising his head) or moves to where there is no pressure which is backwards.

Solution: Ideally, you want your horse to respond to a light push from your seat or a gentle squeeze from your leg. But, for your horse to feel that he can go forward, the reins and your seat must give to and follow his forward movement at the same time you apply your leg aid. Gently push forward from your seat bones as if you want to push the back of your saddle towards the front of your saddle. Next add gentle pressure from your lower leg making sure you don't squeeze in your knees or upper inner thighs. Be careful to not drop your weight heavily into your horse's back as that will cause him to drop his back. When his back is dropped, the parking brake is on. If your horse does not respond immediately to your request, soften your body and then ask again. Focus on getting him to move just one foot. He may have learned to become 'dull' to your aids through previous miscommunication. If this is the case, you can help him to understand by:

- teaching him to respond to voice cues in your ground work exercises (in hand or lunging).

- Taking lunge line lessons from a competent trainer so you can practice applying light aids while the trainer gives your horse cues from the ground.

182

2. Turning

Problem: You ask your horse to circle left, but he continues straight or pushes to the right.

Reason: Your horse can only turn left when he has a left bend in his body and his spine is aligned poll to tail. Asking a horse to turn left when he is bent right creates stress and resistance in his body. He is unbalanced when his neck is over-flexed because his nose is pulled in to the left.

Solution: Apply your inside leg for bend only when your horse's barrel is swinging out. Apply your outside leg to turn only when your horse's weight is off is outside front leg that is when his outside shoulder is moving forward.

At the walk, when your horse has a left bend his barrel swings out as his left hind leg is off the ground and swinging forward. In the next beat, his outside shoulder will swing forward. So,your inside leg at the girth keeps the bend by pushing the barrel out as your inside hip drops and your outside upper leg (thigh) pushes the outside shoulder over when it is coming forward.

At the trot, the correct time to ask your horse to turn left is on the up-beat of your post while he has a left bend. His inside hind and outside front legs are coming forward. His weight is off his outside front leg and his barrel is swinging out. Soften on the down beat and ask again for the turn on the next up beat. You can also gently turn your belly button in on the up beat (don't let your shoulders follow) and straighten on the down beat.

3. Down transitions

Problem: You ask your horse to come down from trot to walk and he pulls down on the reins or flips his head and hollows his back.

Reason: All transitions – including downwards ones - are initiated from the hindquarters so your horse's back is lifted. As your horse steps onto his inside hind leg, you stop your seat from following his movement and create a block through your upper body by inflating your chest. These actions restrict your horse's forward movement without pulling. Leaning back with the upper body or pulling on the reins throw your horse off balance causing resistance. Your horse hollows his back and flips his head up against the pressure to his spine from your driving seat or pulls against your pull from the reins.

Solution: Combine the timing used in up transitions and turning with blocking his forward movement while staying light on his back and without pulling on the reins. Your seat and elbows stop following your horse's movement. If he pulls against your blocking aids then lift and open your chest to create a stronger centre of resistance. Gradually turn him into a small circle until he stops. As soon as you feel him stopping, release your blocking aids. Re-apply them as necessary.

With correct timing of your aids, working with the natural movement of your horse while maintaining balance, suppleness and calmness in your own body, your riding will become fluid and smooth rather than mechanical and rough. Riding will be more enjoyable for both you and your horse.

As your awareness for your own alignment, your horse's alignment and your alignment to each other becomes more consistent, you will eliminate these situations where you feel out of control. Your horse will become more tuned into your seat and leg aids and he will follow your directions more easily and willingly without pulling into the bridle or running through your leg.

Doing the riding exercise given on the following page will help you develop and maintain alignment and open up better communication with your horse through your seat and leg aids.

Exercise – Walk A Straight Line One Step At A Time

If possible, do this exercise with a ground person to give you immediate feedback about your alignment.

1. Sit on your horse with correct, supple and balanced posture ensuring you have both vertical alignment (ears – shoulders – hips – heels) and rectangular alignment (shoulders and hips)..

2. Pick a visual target in the distance to ride towards on a straight line. Have your ground person stand at the end of the line (or ride towards a mirror).

3. Ask your horse to be straight from poll to tail with his nose lined up with the centre of his chest.

4. Open both reins equally and keep both hands on the same plane. Use the reins only to keep his nose in the centre of his chest.

5. Ride towards this target keeping your belly button centred between your horse's ears.

Your horse will naturally drift to the left or the right. As soon as you notice that he is drifting (or your ground person tells you), close your upper leg on the drifting side (eg. left thigh to left shoulder).

Use your upper leg to push the shoulder over only as the shoulder moves forward. This is when the horse's foot is off the ground and he is physically able to move his leg over.

Make sure the opposite upper leg is not gripping or closed or this will block your horse from being able to move away from the pushing leg.

Make sure you do not pull on the reins but continue to use them only as boundaries.

Continue making adjustments, one step at a time, as you walk the length of the straight line.

Have your ground person (or check yourself in the mirror), give you feedback about both your alignment and your horse's.

Repeat this exercise several times. As you rely less on the reins for steering, you will find that your horse responds more quickly and easily to your aids and stays straighter for longer periods of time.

Part 4

YOU ARE NOT ALONE

Experience tells you what to do; confidence allows you to do it.

"~ Stan Smith

Chapter 11 – True Inspirational Stories

My Own Story – A Coach Without Confidence

This book came out of my own journey of losing and regaining my confidence. I have loved horses for as long as I can remember. I found opportunities to be around them whenever I could. I would watch local fall fair horse shows, visit the stabling area at the Royal Winter Fair and the Canadian National Exhibition in Toronto. When I was 13 years old, I started working at a private farm on week-ends. In exchange for some occasional lessons and opportunities to ride one of their ponies, I did the usual farm chores – mucking stalls, sweeping the barn, cleaning and filling water buckets. I didn't start taking formal riding lessons until I was in my early twenties and that was after I bought my first horse. So, I really have lived "green on green equals black and blue". But because I was still in my mid-twenties, I still had some bounce and recovered quickly from the minor injuries I suffered.

I started that first horse, Trooper, by reading a book. I got as far as being able to sit on his back and be lead around before I realized that I probably needed to get help from a professional horse trainer. I was beginning to realize how much I didn't know about horse or riding.

I moved Trooper from my in-law's farm to Stoney Brook Stables, a boarding, training and show barn. It was here that I became interested in showing. Since this was a hunter/jumper barn that was the discipline I focused on. Unfortunately, Trooper was not a hunter "type" horse and I made the painful decision to sell him and buy a horse more suited to my goals. But that's a whole other story ….

While at Stoney Brook Stables, I began teaching beginner and novice level riders and helping to run their schooling shows. This was the beginning of my path to owning my own boarding stable and becoming a full-time professional horse trainer and riding coach. I also did some breeding of sport horses which lead to handling, training, showing youngsters in line (halter) classes and starting them under saddle.

In 2007, I was riding one of my young horses. Dooley was the second foal from my thoroughbred mare, Gemini, and by a Hanoverian stallion, Wellington II. He is a big, gelding – 16.3hh and very solidly built. He had been diagnosed with EPSM (Equine Polysaccharide Myopathy) which is a muscle disease that can be managed through diet and exercise. One of the symptoms of the disease is muscle soreness.

I thought I was managing things well for Dooley as he was doing well and I was riding him without any sign of problems. Until that day in 2007 when he started bucking like a bronc just after we walked away from the mounting block on a long rein. I stayed with him for a few bucks, but we parted ways when he went left to avoid a jump standard and I went right. Being in my 40's, I did not bounce when I hit the ground. It's a long way down from a 16.3hh horse who is bucking with quite a bit of force. I was sore and bruised, but otherwise physically unharmed.

However, my confidence was severely shaken. I wondered why I had not seen or felt the trouble coming. I doubted my ability to read a horse. I doubted myself as a rider and as a trainer. How could I ever trust myself on a horse again if I could be bucked off a horse that I had bred and trained? How could I coach people to ride if I did not have the courage to get on their horses if needed.? A good coach needs to be able to show her students what to do and deal with training issues that are beyond the student's skill set.

Here I was making my living as a full-time riding coach and yet I was dealing with fear so bad that the mere thought of getting on a horse – any horse – caused butterflies in my stomach. I would physically shake at the thought of getting on another horse – even one that I knew well and trusted. I did not trust myself or the horses anymore.

I had a choice to make – find a new career or find a way to overcome my fear and regain my confidence. Since I couldn't imagine myself doing anything else for a living, I simply had to work on rebuilding my confidence. And so my journey began. The information in this book comes from research and practices I did on that journey.

Often, especially at the beginning, my progress was baby steps. But each small step forward gave me a bit more confidence. I developed patience and compassion as well as much more empathy for myself, the horses and the adult clients that I now work with. Ground work became a much bigger part of my training routine. I created a ritual for myself that included lunging a horse – even if it was for just 2 minutes – just to read how that horse was feeling. From the ground, I knew I could see any potential issues and deal with them before getting into the saddle.

I had to do a lot of self-coaching – using visualization, self-talk and other strategies I discuss in the first section of the book. For a long time, I would never ride a horse if I was alone. I needed to know that someone was there watching who could see something I was missing and to reassure me that all was well. Sometimes, I was ok with having a non-horse person (usually my husband) ready to help me and call 911 if necessary. These people were part of my support group.

I always did (and still do) a risk assessment of any riding situation. It is my butt in the saddle so I get to decide what I think is too risky. If I feel a situation will get out of control – either because I am too tense to be able to help calm the horse or the horse is getting too fractious – I will dismount, do some ground work to calm myself and the horse, and then get back on.

I can tell you that the fear never completely goes away. But it rears its head less and less often. I have learned to manage it, recognize the earliest symptoms and developed strategies that work for me to diffuse it.

I am no different to you. If I can do it so can you. Make up your mind. Be determined. Be patient with yourself. Be prepared to push yourself. Have a support team. If you decide to do the work, you can enjoy riding again. Your self-esteem will soar. You are worth it.

Building Trust – Deborah & Nairobi

We are slowly approaching December. This morning as I walk over to the barn there is a hazy hue in the sky, no wind, and a very comfortable temperature. A vest over my sweatshirt is enough to

keep me warm. I feel light and soft in my heart. I can take in some nice satisfying deep breathes and enter the barn feeling relaxed. I am now surrounded by the warmth and happy nickers from our three horses. The one that has the loudest gurgle and has his head over the gate is Nairobi. He always makes eye contact with me when he sees me. His glance always gives me comfort. Always makes me thankful for everything in my life, especially him. Although it all sounds dreamy and romantic, I can assure you that in the beginning of our horse relationship, it was not. Not so long ago, things were much different for both of us.

My husband and I have had horses in our lives now for close to six years. Not long really. But considering we are middle aged, it is quite a significant amount of time. It is a true commitment and one that must be accompanied with lots of passion, time and energy.

Nairobi is the horse that significantly changed my life. Even more than that, he enriched my life. He changed me.

One day early on in our beginnings, Nairobi spooked while in our large loafing barn. He herded his mates and they all galloped out of the barn. This happened just as I was leaving the barn. I barely had time to look back over my shoulder to see two horse's hooves above my shoulders and a bulging chest coming into my head. I was knocked face down by one horse and Nairobi followed through behind her. I was flat on the ground with pounding hooves imprinting their force across my arms, lower back and legs. I remember first the shock and then praying that I would be able to move each limb and my back and be able to stand up. Thankfully, I was able to move and along with a bruised ego and body I left the barn feeling like a fool.

I remember telling my accident to a lady, and her response was simply "Welcome to horse ownership!"

What I also welcomed to my being was fear. I was now really terrified of being around the horses, but specifically Nairobi. He had my number. He knew I needed to know more. And he was right. But how do I cope with my fear ? No one could help me except for me. So I started to research techniques, and look for clinics that specifically dealt with fear and horses. And that is how I found Anne. She was teaching clinics for women dealing with their fear of horses. She was a 6 hour drive away from where I lived. I drove to attend her clinic. Most importantly for me, I needed help on the ground. Groundwork. With what groundwork teaches you, I was able to slowly move from the fear and gain confidence, language, and knowledge.

Nairobi was a young horse with minimal training. There was something about Nairobi that compelled me to commit to myself and to him to learn more. I think that because Anne was helping us to reveal our fears in the clinic format it helped each of us to learn that the fear might not be the enemy after all. It was inaction, staying the same, not changing, or not learning about what our horses needed from us would keep us frozen. What is the point of being around horses if all you want to do is stay the same and stand still?

I had to start from the very beginning which was creating my boundary. My boundary could change, but only when I wanted it to. Once Nairobi understood this boundary in many different scenarios he became more aware of me. Sometimes my boundary was 2 feet around me. Sometimes it was 15 feet around me. But once he knew he knew. This was significant for my own situation as remember he was on top of me at that moment in the barn when I was trampled. He had no regard for me at that moment. So I had to teach him about me. I learned that in order to create my boundary and be safe. I needed some aids. I never entered the barn without a short crop, a halter, and a lead rope. At first it was all very awkward. But slowly, they became second nature. I might add that even though I was learning to establish my boundary I still was a long way from where I wanted to end up. But the point is that all of these groundwork beginnings were the key to unlocking the beginnings of changes in me and how my horse understood me.

I do know how it feels to feel frozen in fear and to overreact out of fear. Learning as much groundwork exercises I could eventually became second nature. In addition, the bonus was having some fun with him Nairobi. What followed was confidence and eventually leadership.

I equate "love" in horse life to respect and connection. There is no greater feeling to me than when I look over at my horse and I look at his hip he turns; I bend away from him. I draw him into me, I look forward and together we walk side by side all the way down to the lower field without a lead or halter. We have left behind his herd mates. He is willing to stay by me. When we arrive at the gate I stop, he stops and he waits.

I open the gate. I return for him and together we pass through the gate into the open field. He turns his head into my core. I tickle his nose hairs softly. I turn to leave him and he looks at me...now he can go off and be Nairobi.

Paralyzing Fear – Faye and Andante

I am standing on the mounting block with my heart racing. Is this going to be a day when I am able to put my left toe into the stirrup iron and swing my right leg over the back of my horse or not?

My name is Faye and my horse is Andante. My story is not so different from a lot of others- up to a point. I have ridden since I was a young teenager and after high school I achieved AHSA accreditation as a coach. But experience alone had not left me with tools big enough to deal with what I was going through on that mounting block.

I need to back up a bit to explain how I had come to this point. Andante, which ironically is a musical term meaning 'medium slow', had a good start in life before I acquired him as a four-year old in the fall of 2003. He was raised by my vet and her family and started under saddle as a 3-year old. He didn't have a lot of experience, but I was certainly capable of bringing along a relatively green horse. I had done it countless times. So we spent that fall and the following spring getting to know each other in the stall and under saddle.

Things went relatively smoothly- we didn't have any issues that were out of the ordinary. That is until our lives changed in June of 2004 when a woman from down the road, as was her custom, let her two Rottweilers out for a morning run without a thought for the rest of the neighbourhood. They tore down the road, spotted Dante and the game was on. They chased him through every fence on our property, over an 8-foot drop to the adjacent property, through fields, swamps and over downed barbed wire fences, then on to a paved secondary road. At this point my husband, Jack, and I were on his trail and the dogs gave up their sport. But Dante was beyond noticing any of that. As far as he was concerned he was still running for his life.

We caught up with him on a woods road about 4 miles from home. By some miracle he only had a few minor scrapes- but his mind was fried. It took all my skill to calm him down to the point where I could get close enough to attach a lead and take him home again. I am sure that I was shaking as badly as he was. Following this I interacted with him as usual, but gave him a bit of time to settle and then treated him like I was starting a totally green horse again. I was in the saddle again by mid-July, but I could count on him starting or spooking at something during every ride. Inversion became his middle name.

That fall Chris Irwin gave his first clinic in Nova Scotia and I grabbed the opportunity to audit. I was fascinated by the concept that Chris put forward. At last- someone who could read the body language of the horse and use the same shapes in his own body to send messages back that they could understand. Using the pushing, drawing and blocking energies and alignment, he was 'speaking horse'. I witnessed positive changes in horse after horse (along with their riders and handlers) that Chris worked with, and I was hooked! I was sure that this could help Dante. Oh-and I bought him a pony for Christmas! Dante was the first horse that I had kept without a companion and I felt that having a herd mate might help him relax at least while at pasture.

For a multitude of reasons I do not get in much riding over the winter months, so I was very eager to get going again the following spring. Not a lot had changed. Dante was still apprehensive under saddle and not even totally relaxed while at pasture-even with his buddy. Any sudden movement by anything feathered or furry set him off. We live in a rural area and birds large and small, squirrels, rabbits, cats, a dog and a multitude of waterfowl on our pond all became potential predators.

We were doing rather decent 20-meter circles one evening in early May when a grouse took off scarcely 20 feet away from us. Dante wasn't into identifying the threat- he was out of there. He did a quick spin and headed up the driveway and across the road where he found yet another woods road. Unfortunately I was flat on my back in the back field where he had executed the spin. There had been heavy equipment working there over the previous summer and fall and it was just like hitting concrete. I will mention that my head hit the ground hard, too and if I had not been wearing a helmet, the outcome would have been very different. I picked myself up and Jack and I headed off on a search for my black horse once again.

Dante only made it about 2 miles this time, and amazingly the only apparent damage was a broken rein, so I was able to lead him back and get him settled in his stall. Then my husband drove me to the local hospital to have my wrist set.

199

I was strictly forbidden to ride while my wrist healed, and in-hand work with my non-dominant left hand only wasn't going to happen. But we WERE able to construct a round pen, so soon Dante and I headed there. I had many weeks to round pen Dante while waiting impatiently for the break to heal.

By this time I had audited a few more Chris Irwin clinics but had not participated myself. I had a general idea of what to look for and how to shape my body but without the assistance of an experienced coach I know that I wasn't doing everything right. The good news was that I wasn't doing everything wrong either! Dante responded to my efforts and the round pen became his safe haven- he loved working in there. So when I got the green light to ride again I started out in the round pen. It was good for both of us. We soon graduated to the big outdoor arena and finally made some progress until the game was called by old man winter again.

The following year I continued to do ground work with Dante. We always started with some correct in-hand work while making our way back to the area where my round pen and ring are. This was followed by round pen work or longing. The under saddle work was coming along, too. Then while I was mounting him in the arena one day a pheasant took off (they make a LOT of noise) and Dante bolted. I had my left toe in the stirrup but was not completely in the saddle. He dashed to the opposite end of the ring and did a 180 degree turn while my momentum carried me into the 2" thick planks of the fence. I didn't get up quite so quickly this time. Once again I feel that a helmet saved my head from serious injury and I was lucky to get off with a broken rib and many sore muscles, but at this point I lost MY confidence. We were a great pair- hardly an ounce of confidence between the two of us.

I did recognize that I was not afraid of my horse- that never entered the equation. But I didn't bounce as well as I used to and my fear was of being injured again. And fear is very debilitating. I continued to do ground work and participated in a few Chris Irwin clinics. As well I am blessed to have as my closest friend another horse-crazed individual who was also attending the same clinics with her horse and she was a wonderful support for me.

Emotionally I went through a lot. Should I keep working with horses? Would I ever have enough nerve to ride again? Should I sell Dante and get a safer mount? I owed it to my family to consider the consequences if I had a serious injury.

My decision was to not make a hasty decision. I did consider selling Dante, and I was of two schools of thought here. Firstly it was possible that a very confident rider might be able to work him through his issues. But there was also the possibility that another rider could be the one to get seriously injured and that was unthinkable. Plus if that happened he would probably have ended up in a can of dog food- also unacceptable. So I decided to give myself a break. I didn't have a timetable. He had been 'injured' on my watch and I felt that it was my responsibility to make things right again. My only agenda was to heal myself and my horse, mentally and spiritually as well as physically. He was responding very well to my using equine body language and de-stressing exercises with him, so I would continue doing that and play it by ear.

And that is what I did. I went an entire year without riding. I continued to work with my Dante at every opportunity and tried my best to use the skills that I was still learning and honing, to make a difference in both of us. And slowly it did. There were days when I could ride and still days when I thought I could but climbed down off the mounting block with no guilt or negative feelings- it just didn't feel right to ride.

It has been a journey, and today Dante and I are a team. I had to prove myself to him and to earn his trust and he had to do the same with me. Over the years I also had to convince my husband a few times that Dante wasn't a dangerous horse, but a victim on the lookout for the next predator. There was a period when I had to vow that I would not ride unless Jack was on the property. I was willing to do whatever it took. I knew that we had made the grade the day that I saw Jack's truck leave the yard while I was riding- we were there! I asked Jack what had changed his mind about Dante and he summed it up in two words- his eye. It had changed so much that even a non-horse person could detect it. His eye was soft and quiet and Dante's whole persona now exuded trust. People who see us as we are now without knowing our history often comment on what a solid, confident horse he is. That is food for the soul.

The journey continues. Over the past few years we have been fortunate to have Anne Gage visit us on several occasions to conduct clinics. She is fluent in the language of Equus as well as being a gifted coach. Having had issues herself has given her empathy for what others are going through, though nothing gets by her. Her own confidence is infectious and her sense of humour keeps everything flowing. Dante and I willingly throw ourselves into her hands and try anything that she asks us to do during a lesson. We always leave on a high note with something to think about…until the next time.

The issues that I have had with Dante have had a profound effect on me. I have traveled down paths that I might not even have known existed before. It is so disheartening when your dream horse turns into your worst nightmare. I have chosen to make lemonade with my lemons- and it is very good lemonade. Being the horse that he is, I have had to be there 110% for Dante and we have hammered out a wonderful relationship because of it. He has made me step up to the plate and give him even more than I knew that I had. And I have to agree with the saying that sometimes 'we do not get the horse that we want, but we do get the horse that we need'.

Building Trust from the Ground ~ Kelly and Ithica

As an adult rider who returned to riding after several years off, I was experiencing an almost continuous low-level fear and paralysis response occurring while working with all but the most sedate of horses. When I purchased Ithaca, an athletic and extroverted green Thoroughbred mare, my dream of working with my horse in ease and harmony seemed almost out of reach. No matter how much I learned about 'what' to do from excellent sources (clinics, coaches, books, etc), I could not seem to 'turn off' my fear response. I also had an unrecognized and untreated physical imbalance that was causing my aids while riding to be 'incongruent' despite my best efforts.

Faced with these physical and emotional incongruencies from her owner, Ithaca began to escalate her 'no' responses. It was at that point that I made a conscious decision to focus our time together on ground work exclusively.

Ithaca and I had previously established the fundamentals of body language through in-hand and lunging exercises, but I intuitively felt a different approach was needed for us. After years of working on horse farms without sufficient knowledge of horse language, I had been hurt many times because 'I didn't see it coming'. I had a strong sense that I needed to work with Ithaca at liberty in the arena and take things back to basics.

Instead of focusing all my attention on Ithaca's behavior and adjusting my cues accordingly, I entered the arena with only one criterion – respect my space. I moved however I liked and I allowed Ithaca to express herself however she liked…as long as it was 'out there'. After some time of this I noticed a shift. Instead of getting a shot of adrenalin when Ithaca spooked or 'acted up', I began to feel the playfulness and exuberance in her actions. From my safe distance her expressions were beautiful not scary.

This change in perception allowed me to stay present in the moment much better, which in turn empowered me to feel safe with less physical distance between us. When fear was not crippling me and I was fully engaged in the moment, I did not feel like a sitting duck anymore!

Once my internal reality shifted to one of harmony, my communication with Ithaca became much subtler and softer. I have been working consistently with a chiropractor and am doing exercises that have really helped with my riding, but I will continue with consistent ground work as the primary avenue for relationship building with Ithaca.

Recognize What Isn't Working ~ Alison and Be

Have you ever felt completely useless and ineffective with your horse? Have you ever felt that you were completely and utterly in over your head? I have and it was the best thing that could have happened for my horse and me.

I hit my personal rock bottom as a mature rider. I had ridden and showed as a youth but horses were put aside for the business of growing up and I didn't return to them until my 30's. I had been riding, happily for a few years when I ran into trouble with a new horse. The first time I tried to ride her I sensed something wasn't right. She would walk a few steps and then stop. No amount of encouragement would make her go forward. Frustration turned to fear when she would respond by backing up. Was she going to rear? Buck? I hadn't ridden in more than a year, since the birth of my daughter. I was no longer confident in my skills and as the stay at home mother of a toddler I couldn't risk being injured.

The vet came out and said she needed her teeth floated. Ah! I thought I had solved the problem but no. The next time I tried to ride her, same thing. I contacted Anne Gage after reading an article on horse body language in Horse Canada. The first thing she identified was that not only did my saddle not fit correctly but she had a sore back indicating that she had been previously ridden with an ill-fitting saddle. She was a horse in pain.

But that wasn't all. Not only did she not like me, she didn't respect me. She wasn't a 'bad' horse but she wasn't easy either. I certainly wouldn't trust her. She was a very difficult horse to catch so I was in the habit of bribing her with treats to come to me. When I did have her Anne pointed out how she pushed me around and I didn't even realize it! She was also a very sensitive horse and my body language was often challenging her, provoking her. She was suffering from Previous Training Stress Disorder. I didn't know what happened in the nine years of her life before she came to me but it was clear that whatever it was had left her traumatized and mistrustful of people.

I began the long process of retraining, rehabilitating this horse. I learned how to 'listen' to her by reading her body language and how to communicate with her in a meaningful way with my own body language. I don't have an indoor arena so I faced many limitations on how much and what kind of work we could do. But I have the luxury of having my horse at home and although I'm a 'busy mom' I found the consistency of my groundwork, just minutes a day, while feeding, grooming or just 'hanging out' was all it took to help her begin to come around and start to see me as a reliable leader and worthy of her trust.

It hasn't all been easy. There have been moments when I've been in tears because I just can't seem to grasp a new skill. Usually, it's because my body isn't doing what I want it to. It's important to take care of yourself. Acupuncture, meditation and Qigong are what I find useful to help balance my body and mind but there are many other ways to do this too.

Patience is essential. It's been easier for me to be patient with my horse than with myself but when I look back over the past couple of years I can see how much I've improved. I know that with time, the things that challenge me today will be overcome.

I have held on to the long-term goal of being able to ride my horse, both of us relaxed, in open fields. I haven't forgotten it but what is first and foremost in my mind on any given day is what is happening in the moment. There are many steps to achieving that goal and I realize that we both have a lot to learn if we're going to do it right. I love my new knowledge and the meaningful relationship I'm developing with my horse as a result.

So when you are completely and utterly stuck and so frustrated you don't know what to do, rejoice. For when you recognize that what you've been doing isn't working and your mind opens up to meet the challenges – your full potential is about to be released.

"Don't wait until everything is just right. It will never be perfect. There will always be challenges, obstacles and less than perfect conditions. So what. Get started now. With each step you take, you will grow stronger and stronger, more and more skilled, more and more self-confident and more and more successful."

~ Mark Victor Hansen

Chapter 12 – Closing Words and Thoughts

Take Action

The quote above says it well. If you have worked through the exercises in this book, you should have the outline of a plan to help you build your confidence. If you haven't done the exercises, what are you waiting for? The best time to start is now. Overcoming your fear begins with taking a step – action overcomes fear. No one can do it for you.

You are on a journey. Be kind to yourself. You are a work in progress and so is your horse. As you go through the process of change, remember to keep the fun and passion in what you are doing. After all, you didn't become involved with horses to add more stress to your life!

Remember also to recognize, share and celebrate your successes no matter how small they may be. A good horse trainer recognizes and rewards the horse's "try". Do this for yourself as well.

Building your confidence requires that you increase your understanding of yourself and your horse. The additional benefit is that your relationship with your horse will improve and you will develop a stronger bond based on mutual trust and respect. Who knows; you might even find – as I and others have - that this knowledge and new level of confidence positively affects other relationships in your life. But, that's for another book.

In the meantime …

Enjoy the ride.

~

What If?

It seems that fears are all based on these things: illusion and future thinking, with a side order of 'What if.'

'What if that truck turns suddenly into our lane'

 'What if I'm all alone at age 80?'

What if? What if? What if?

Yes, fears must be respected and learned about, but they must not paralyze us, or lure us into a half-life of being afraid all the time. I liked to think of my fears being driven away in a Rolls Royce (for it is true that once you face a fear, it loses all of its stuffing, and will sit quietly in the back seat and do as it's told.)

 I feel that fears drive us away from our true selves--innocent beings. I used to live in denial of my fears, and try to cover them up with a 'happy face.'

I now see that my greatest growth is happening with an acceptance of my fears, of giving them voices and learning new ways to deal with them.

~ Anonymous

The Serenity Prayer

God grant me the serenity
to accept the things I cannot change;
courage to change the things I can;
and wisdom to know the difference.

Living one day at a time;
Enjoying one moment at a time;
Accepting hardships as the pathway to peace;
Taking, as He did, this sinful world
as it is, not as I would have it;
Trusting that He will make all things right
if I surrender to His Will;
That I may be reasonably happy in this life
and supremely happy with Him
Forever in the next.
Amen.

--Reinhold Niebuhr

About The Author

Anne Gage has had a lifelong love of horses and riding. How she acquired the "horse lover's syndrome" is unknown. As a child, she had to be content with horse books, movies and toys. As a teenager, her riding career began as she worked in exchange for occasional, informal lessons at a private stable.

Anne bought her first horse, started formal riding lessons and began showing in her early twenties. With a passion for teaching and a dream of having her own farm, Anne pursued opportunities that lead to a career in coaching and, eventually, breeding, training and showing sport horses at her own farm.

Her hunger for knowledge took her to a clinic given by Chris Irwin. Recognizing that he was teaching a better way to be with horses, Anne studied with him through his Train the Trainer program. She is now recognized as one of the top Chris Irwin Certified Trainers in North America.

Since then, Anne has continued to learn and has studied the techniques of Linda Tellington Jones (TTEAM® and TTOUCH®), and Peggy Cummings (Connected Riding®) as well as learning more about science based equine behaviour.

Anne's mission is to help horses and humans be calm, confident and connected - together. She works with adults and their horses to improve their confidence through better horsemanship and riding skills.

Certified in groundwork, riding, Equine Sports Psychology, Equine Assisted Personal Development, as a Life Coach and NLP Practitioner, Anne offers something not provided by traditional horse trainers and coaches - an understanding of horse psychology, body language, and bio-mechanics, and fundamental riding skills as well as the physical and emotional challenges that affect the confidence and skill level (both on the ground and in the saddle) of adult riders.

Through lessons, workshops and clinics, Anne helps people to:

- ride with confidence;
- bring the fun & enjoyment back into their time with horses;
- become the rider their horse deserves.

Anne offers both in person and distance lessons and is available to give clinics, workshops and seminars for all levels of horse's and horse people. For more information, visit www.annegage.com

Bibliography

Au, Pamela J.G. <u>Zen and the Horse: Body, Mind and Spiritual Unity Through the Art of Equitation.</u> United States: Xlibris Corporation, 2002

Dorrance, Tom. <u>True Unity: Willing Communication Between Horse and Human.</u> Sanger: Give-It-A-Go-Enterprises, 1987

Hunt, Ray. <u>Think Harmony with Horses: An In-depth Study of Horse/Man Relationship.</u> Bruneau: Give-It-A-Go Books, 1998

Irwin, Chris. <u>Dancing with Your Dark Horse: How Horse Sense Helps Us Find Balance, Strength & Wisdom</u>. New York: Marlow & Company, 2005

Irwin, Chris. <u>Horses Don't Lie: The Magic of Horse Whispering</u>. Winnipeg: Great Plains Publications, 1998

Jeffers, Susan. <u>Feel the Fear and Do It Anyway.</u> New York: Fawcett Columbine, 1987

Marks, Kelly et al. <u>Ride with Confidence! Practical and Inspirational Advice to Help You Deal with Your Fear and Enjoy Your Riding</u>. Cincinnati: David and Charles, 2004

Rashid, Mark. <u>Horsemanship Through Life.</u> Provo: Spring Creek Press, 2005

Rashid, Mark. <u>Horses Never Lie: The Horse of Passive Leadership.</u> Provo: Spring Creek Press, 2000

Webb, Wyatt. <u>It's Not About the Horse: It's About Overcoming Fear and Self-Doubt.</u> United States: Hay House Inc., 2003

Webb, Wyatt. <u>What To Do When You Don't Know What To Do: Common Horse Sense.</u> United States: Hay House Inc., 2006

Resources

Website:

www.annegage.com – Confident Horsemanship with Anne Gage. Author of "Confident Rider Confident Horse". Contributing writer to Horse Canada Magazine. Training for horses and humans. Ground Work and Riding lessons and clinics. Equine Assisted Personal Development workshops. Links to my articles, videos, and online shop.

Facebook:

Free Group:
www.facebook.com/groups/confidenthorsmanshipcommunity

Page: www.facebook.com/confidenthorsemanshp

Email:

anne@confidenthorsemanship.com